Economics of Hotel Management

A.M. Sheela
Reva Institute of Science & Technology Studies
Bangalore

NEW AGE INTERNATIONAL (P) LIMITED, PUBLISHERS
(formerly Wiley Eastern Limited)
New Delhi • Bangalore • Chennai • Guwahati • Hyderabad
Jalandhar • Kolkata • Lucknow • Mumbai • Ranchi
Visit us at **www.newagepublishers.com**

PUBLISHING FOR ONE WORLD

Published by New Age International (P) Ltd., Publishers
Fourth Edition : 2002
Reprint : 2007

ISBN : 81-224-1419-2

The Law Publishers

C-07-08-1890

3 4 5 6 7 8 9 10

Printed in India at Sandeep Press, Delhi.

PUBLISHING FOR ONE WORLD

NEW AGE INTERNATIONAL (P) LIMITED, PUBLISHERS
(formerly Wiley Eastern Limited)
4835/24, Ansari Road, Daryaganj, New Delhi - 110002
Visit us at **www.newagepublishers.com**

Dedicated to
my
Parents
(Late) Mary Margaret
(Late) M.D. Anthony Raj

Preface

The field of economics encompasses the study of the entire economic system — both at the micro and macro level. Hotel economics is one such area where the subject matter of economics has gained its growth in obtaining for the hotel industry needed aspects, right from its initiation, establishment, and growth. The hotel industry though considered to be a service sector has proved its might in different dimensions — providing employment, revenue to the government and also acting as a promoter of culture by developing the most vital industry which is tourism. Tourism has emerged as a most instrumental phenomenon in the economic and social development of the society. It also acts as a subsidiary in providing accommodation to the tourist who visit the country — by providing the most luxurious accommodation to the one like the motel where basic necessities are provided even to a poor tourist. It is seen that the industry as a whole generates not only a sizeable percentage of employment but also contributes to the GNP of a country. The importance of this field has grown over the years leading many institutes to provide education in this field.

The thought of writing a textbook on Hotel economics originated from the author's experience as a teacher in the subject. Since it was a foray into a new field of economics, it needed immense effort to provide the students with a better understanding of the subject, the conflux of various concepts into the syllabi, total lack of textbooks in the subject has posed great difficulty not only to students but also to teachers. This strengthened the conviction to pen a book on the subject.

The main objective of the book is :

- To educate the students in undstanding the concepts of economics which helps in the study of hotel management?

- It also tries to link the interrelated dimension of economics into the tourism and hotel industry.

The author has endeavoured to bring in the various dimensions of economic concepts related to the study of hotel management. Through suitable examples, it provides an insight into the subject matter of economics, which is not only theory based but which helps in day-to-day business operations.

The book has ten chapters. They throw light on the efficacy on the subject matter of economics both at the micro level and macro level in the hotel industry. The discussions have been corroborated with suitable figures illustrations, examples and flow charts, which simplifies the understanding of the theme.

The author is heavily indebted to many libraries like the Indian Social Institute, ISEC, 'Equations' and others which helped in providing valuable research material.

Grateful thanks to Dr. Lalith, professor, University of Agricultural sciences for his constant support and guidance. The author wishes to specially thank Ms. Adithi of Equations for the timely help. Wish to thank many friends like Mr. Surender, Mr. Samuel, Mr. Shashi Sharma, Ms. Deepa, Mr. Srinivasa and Mr. Nagaraj. She also wishes to thank New Age International Publishers and Director Mr. K.K. Gupta for providing me with an opportunity to publish my first work through their company. I would sincerely thank Mr. V.R. Babu New Age International Publishers, Bangalore in this regard.

I hope this book will be of immense help to hotel management students, and also business management students. Valuable suggestions for improvements from fellow teachers and students will be highly appreciated.

A.M. Sheela

Contents

1
The Hotel Industry

1.1 ROLE OF ECONOMICS IN THE HOTEL INDUSTRY

Economics is not only the study of wealth as stated by Adamsmith, or a field confining itself to the study of human behaviour, which traces a relationship between unlimited ends and scare means as referred by lionel Robbins. It is a field of study which encompasses the study of human behaviour in relation to money. Over the years the vast expanse of the subject of economics has helped in varied fields both micro and macro. One such field is Managerial Economics.

Managerial Economics is very closely connected with the hotel industry. The hotel industry though considered a service sector, providing service in the form of food and accomodation to its guests is considered as an industry whose main aim is also to make profits, though this may change at times.

The hoteliering sector consists of different categories of hotels—namely the five star three star and other categories. These differenciate the hotels based on the service of varied types, which are provided to the guest for instance the hotel may provide food accomodation and other services—which include a luxury room with a television, telephone, ticketing, transport etc. It is seen here that customers have to incur a price for the use of all services.

The subject of economics helps the sector in various ways right from the time of initiation which leads to its establishment, and growth. For instance the decision of starting a hotel itself involves decision making to analyse the need for opening a hotel the cost to be incurred, the choice of selecting the right place to open an hotel, also plays a role in its growth. The type of facilities offered, the number of rooms to be built, all these decision have to possess the need and timing, for which the concept of economiccs is utilised.

The production activity involves the types of cuisine to be prepared each day. The type which is more preferred by guests. The cost incurred to be setup the hotel has also to be calculated. The guiding principles of economics enables the hotel industry to get not only profits but tries to avoid loss and to survive in the competitive situation.

The cost of production also plays an important role in the continued survival of an industry. Any business venture needs financial resources for its sustenance and growth. In incurring expenditure on different inputs the hotel industry has also to check for the principles of cost benefit to enter in to production activity. Profits act as the main motivator in initiating a business. Though the primary motive of profit need not necessarily be the principle objective of the business. Whatever may be the production line, a certain percentage of profit is necessary as it acts as a seed money for further investment and also a reward for the entrepreneurs risk bearing ability. Profits in the hotel industry depends to a large extent of guest arrivals. In a given year when tourist inflow would be abundant leading to a greater demand for accomodation, the entrepreneurs has to use this opportunity to either modify service charges in a way. So that he obtains a large flow. Like- wise in an off season when there are less number of tourists, the rent has to be slightly increased, so that he makes up for the loss incurred through unutilised facilities.

In the hotel industry, also there is stiff competition among the same categories of hotels in the form of accommodation. They provide the facilities they have and the price is charged for the service incurred. Here or the name plays an important role.

The hotel industry is only a subsidiary of the main service sector which is tourism, which relates to the flow of tourist within the country from outside. The macro economic concepts help the tourism industry to grow over a longer period of time. The economic policies both fiscal and monetary affect tourism industry, to a great extent. The effective function of tourism depends on appropriate decisions in accordance to the changes in the govt. policy.

It is thus seen that the subject matter of economics plays an important role in the effective functioning of the service sector which is tourism and its subsidiary unit, which is the hotel industry.

1.2. HISTORICAL BACKGROUND

The advent of industrial revolution lead to rapid changes in field of tourism also. People started moving to different places to seek change. The religious pilgrimage also helped people to travel far and wide. Monastries and cathedrals started to welcome tourists and provided free accommodation to them. Though by the 15th century, INNS were opened in many countries like England and France, it was only in the 17th and 18th century that these facilities expanded. Most inns were located at places where coaches changed horses and passengers took rest to have refreshment or to spend a night before continuing their onward journey.

When the railways appeared on scene the traveling time began to reduce. The inns went out of business. The 'inns' took the name of 'taverns'. In 1634 Samuel cole opened the first tavern. By the end of the 17th century, taverns became popular meeting places where people met for food and entertainment.

The 'Hotels' emerged from the taverns by a change in name. The residence of rich were known as 'hotel' in France. Public places like the town hall were also known as the hotel. David Law opened the the first prototype modern hotel in 1774. This lead to the gradual expansion of hotels in Britain and other places. In 1820 the first hotel appeared in Switzerland. However it as only after two decades that the word 'hotel' came to recognized as a place where people stayed for the night and took their food on payment.

The history of the modern hotel industry was initiated by entrepreneurs who wanted to enhance their wealth and fame on a grand scale. The early 1900's saw the establishment of the Plaza hotel in New York city. Built in 1903, this hotel was the first of its kind with its exquisite ballrooms, suites and public areas. The other famous hotels of those times included the Ritz Carlton and the Statler chains.

Conrad Hilton was the first successful hotelier to start a chain of hotels after the first world war. He acquired the 3000 room

Stevens hotel (now called the Chicago Hilton), followed by the purchase of the Palmer House in Chicago, the Plaza and Waldorf-Astoria in New York city, during the second world war. He also formed the Hilton group of hotels in 1946. At the same time Henderson started the Sheraton group, and K Wilson formed the Holiday-Inn chain.

The hotel industry however declined in its growth during the great depression, but the pioneering hoteliers like Texas Oliman, Conrad Hilton were not discouraged. Their competition was in fact very intense. The 1960's saw the growth of the Hyatt group. The Hyatt group set an example with their expert marketing and operation style. The 1970's saw the development of Hilton, Sheraton, and West-in-Corporations.

1.3. THE LODGING INDUSTRY

The word 'lodging' refers to a place where accommodation and food is provided to visitors or tourists, on the payment of money. A knowledge of the classification of the lodging industry is necessary to understand its organization.

There are various types of facilities to the guests by the industry, they are classified based on the type of lodging provided, market orientation, commercial operations location, function and others. They are :

TYPES OF LODGING PROPERTIES

a. Hotels
b. Motels
c. All-suites
d. Motor inns and lodges
e. Corporate education centers
f. Inns
g. Lodges
h. Bed and break fasts
i. Hostels
j. Resorts
k. Condominiums and time shares
l. Life care

Market Orientation

a. Residential

Center city

a. hotels
b. all-suites
c. condominiums
d. life care

b. Commercial

1. Center city

a. hotels
b. all suites
c. motor inns and lodges
d. corporate`education centers
e. condominiums

2. Sub Urban

a. hotels
b. motels
c. all suites
d. motor inns and motor lodges
e. corporate education centers
f. inns
g. lodges
h. bed and break fast
i. hostels
j. resorts
k. condominiums

3. Airport

a. hotels
b. motels
c. all-suites
d. motor inns and motor lodges
e. condominiums

4. Highways

a. motels
b. all-suites
c. motor inns and motor lodges
d. inns
e. lodges

f. bed and break fast
g. hostels
h. resorts

Hotel : Hotel is often referred to as a 'home away from home'. It is the place where the tourist stops being a traveler and becomes the guest. A hotel usually offers a full range of accommodations and services, which may include, suites, public dining, and banquet facilities, lounge, and entertainment facilities. The main characteristic feature which sets a hotel apart from other types of accommodation centers, is the completeness of facilities and services available.

In addition to the availability of various general services, a variety of other services like auto, rental, airline ticketing, tour, reservation booking, postal services and others. The size of hotels range from twenty to more than two thousand rooms. Hotels are found in center city, suburban, and airport locations.

Thus the main functions of hotel include:

- Providing living accommodation.
- Supplying food, drink, for immediate consumption.
- Having transportation
- Recreational, entertainment facilities
- Any other functions incidental or ancillary to these functions.

Motels: Motels offer guest limited range of services, which may include reservations, vending machines, swimming pools, and cable television. The size of property averages from ten to fifty units. Motels are usually in suburban highways and airport locations, guests at times stay overnight or a few days. They are mainly used by travellers.

All-Suites: A new addition to the lodging industry, it offers a wide range of services, which may include reservation, living room, and separate bedroom, kitchenette, public dining room, and room service. Cable television, video cassette players and recorders, speciality shops, personal services, swimming pool, transportation. The size of the property can range from fifty to over hundred units. This type of property is usually found in center-city, sub urban and airport locations.

Bed and Breakfast: This European concept is now a mainstay in the United States. Bed and breakfast popularly B and B offer the guest limited services, including reservations, and continental breakfast. Size of the property ranges from one to twenty five rooms. The length of the stay can be for a night or a few days. This cottage industry captures the very essence of hospitality providing rooms, food and beverage and fellowship. If offers inexpensive service to it customers. It helps in exposing the local history and customs.

Hostels: These offer bare necessities of shelter. Guests have to provide themselves their own bed, linen, food, and other essentials. A reservation service is offered, membership in the hostel group is encouraged. Overnight fees are nominal. Check-in and check-out and length of the stay are monitored.

Resorts: They offer the guest full range of services which include reservation, suites, dining, and banquet facilities, lounge and entertainment facilities, cable television, speciality shopping, personal services, swimming pools and other recreational facilities, transportation and a coordinator to monitor activities. These resorts are usually located in suburban highways, near hill stations, tourist spots near a sea, etc. The resort is considered an end destination, complete with full range of social activities. Rest, relaxation, recreation are the main focus of resorts.

Floatels: These are referred to as 'floating hotels'. These type of hotels are situated on the surface of the water-rivers or lakes. House boats are good examples of floatels. They have all necessary facilities, which include food, accommodation. The guest usually stays for a period of time. There are various floatels in operation.

Condominiums: These type of properties offer a guest a wide range of services, which include public dining, social activities, speciality shops, personal services (laundry, cleaning, hair care and maid service), recreational facilties. They are usually located in the sub urban areas.

Motor inns: These properties offer the guest a medium range of services, which may include reservations, public dining, and banquet facilities, lounge and entertainment areas, room service, cable television, meeting rooms, personal services, swimming pools, and other recreational facilities and ground transportation to and from an airport. The size of the property ranges from one hundred to three hundred fifty rooms. Motor inns and motor lodges are found in suburban, airport and highway locations. The guest can stay overnight or for several days.

Corporate Education Centers: They offer the guest a complete range of services, dining room with waiter or self service, recreational facilities, exercise room, tennis, basket ball, indoor pool and jogging track and full classroom facilities. This is a leisure package offered to the educational trainees. These facilities may be available for the general public when the corporate trainees leave. The property ranges from one hundred to five hundred rooms. They are less in number and they are located near corporate headquarters, in remote locations.

Inns: Started in the 17th century, inns offer the guest a full range of services, which may include reservations, suites, public dining, and banquet facilities, lounges, and entertainment facilities, room services, cable television, meeting rooms, personal services, and other recreational services, transportation facilities. The size of an inn can vary from twenty five to three hundred fifty rooms. They are found in suburban and highway locations. The length of guest stay can vary from a day to a number of days. Inns are found in suburban and highways. An inn usually is a setting with historical overtones. An inn can also be a social center for a small size community.

Lodges: A lodge offers the guest medium services, which may include reservations, suites, public dining, lounge and entertainment facilities, specialty, shops and other recreational facilities. The lodges are usually fairly small compared to other accommodations. The fee charged is usually nominal. The guest stay is usually for a short period or can be for a longer period of time. They are located in urban areas and suburbs and on highways.

Cruise lines: These are tourist ships, which provide food, accommodation and various entertainment facilities to its guests, on board. The ships sail to different destinations in and around a particular region. It provides different types of accommodation to its guests. Small ships hold around 100 guests. The bigger ships hold around 200 to 300 guests. It is seen that most of the cruise lines are in operation in the United States of America, the

Caribbean Islands, Europe, and some countries and islands in Asia. There are around 285 cruise lines in operation. The famous cruise lines include the Royal Caribbean international travels, the Crystal Cruises, which has three ships sailing all around the world.

Airport hotels: They are situated near airports. Generally depend on airline passengers and airline crew. They offer food and accommodation to passengers who are on their transit journey. They offer package deals and discounts. The example of airport hotels would be that of centaur hotel and Santacruz hotel, mumbai.

The hotels are also classified on the basis on different plans. Which provide different kinds of service to guest and which are minimal in nature.

1. The Continental plan
2. The European plan
3. The American plan
4. Bermuda Plan

Continental plan: Includes room tariff and a continental breakfast.

European plan: Includes only room tariff which is exclusive of food.

American plan: Known as the pension plan or plan of half board, it includes room tariff, breakfast, and any one of the two meals.

Bermuda plan: Includes the room tariff and morning tea.

1.4. HOTELIERING IN INDIA

Indias historical past, its cultural heritage and its varied landscape and terrain have attracted travellers from time immemorial. People from different parts of the world have been attracted to India for its natural endowments, religious and spiritual heritage. These tourist travelled from place to place using the bare minimum transport and stayed in 'Shastras' also called the common rest houses, for shelter and cater on the hotels or inns came into the scene.

The first Indian owned hotel was the one built by Jamshedji Tata in Bombay in 1903 called the 'The Taj Mahal'. M.S. Oberoi was the first man to think of running hotels. The oberoi chain of hotels in India is known after his name. The first Oberoi international in New Delhi was started in 1965. The spencer group were another famous group of pioneers who started the Blue Mountain hotel at Kotagiri in 1942 and Savoy Hotel at Ootacamund in 1943. But still when India became independent there were only a few hotels in India operated by the British and Swiss families.

After independence, the government of India realized the importance of hotels for the development of tourism business. But not many business men in India were willing to invest money in hotel keeping which was often considered not a respectable profession by the business community. Since the private sector was reluctant in hotels, the government of India stepped into building hotels where ever needed. The Ashok hotel in New Delhi was the first one to built in 1956 in the public sector. The hotel was built in a record time of one year, this included a convention hall to seat 2000 people. The department of tourism, government of India decided to set up a hotel classification committee to upgrade the services of hotels. The hotels with most comforts were awarded five or four star ratings. Hotels with modest facilities were categorized as three, two and one star properties, subsequently, creating a five star deluxe category. Hotels were also classified on the basis of size-hotels with less than 25 rooms were called small hotels. Hotels, which had twenty five to ninety nine rooms were called medium hotels. Hotels which had 100 to 300 rooms were called large hotels. Hotels with rooms more than 300 were called very large hotels. The classification process helped in standardizing the services of the hotels. Till recently the goverment of India fixed the tariff of approved hotels on the basis of their standards. The practice has since been given up and now the market forces of demand and supply determine the price of a room in a hotel.

The better hotels in India have high occupancy by foreign visitors who pay in foreign exchange, which is good for the economy of the country. Realising the importance of the hotels, the goverment offered a few concessions to hoteliers and travel agents. For instance the profit earned in foreign exchange are free from income tax. The percentage ranging upto 50 per cent. Hoteliering has been given the status of an industry, which implies that it will get the same preference as an export industry gets.

On the other hand the government imposes such high taxes on hoteliering does not remain very profitable. For instance; the Central Goverment has imposed an expenditure tax of 20 per cent on all the services of a hotel with a room tariff of Rs. 1200 and above. State Governments too have imposed their own luxury taxes of 10 to 10 per cent. In some states the customs pays 50 per cent of the bill as taxes.

The major Indian hotel chains include the five important ones:

1. Ashok Hotel run by the Indian development Corporation (ITDC) has 35 hotels and 3000 rooms also runs restaurants in foreign countries like Russia and New Zealand.
2. Oberoi Hotel chains — has 26 hotels four in India, twelve in abroad. They have started a second chain of budget hotels called Trident and novotel groups.
3. Welcom Group has 21 hotels in India.
4. Taj Group owned by the Tatas, has 28 hotels in India, 15 overseas. They taj group has also started the second chain of budget hotels call gateway hotels.
5. Air India has 4 major hotels, two in Bombay and one in Srinagar and Delhi called Centaur hotels.

To protect the interest of the hotels and hoteliering, Indian hotels have their representative organization with head Quarters in New Delhi called the Federation of hotels and restaurants associations of India (FHRAI) with regional offices in Calcutta, Bombay, and Chennai. The objective of the federation are to upgrade the professional standards of hotels and to for the hotel industry a fair deal from the government.

Apart from the above mentioned hotels which are star rated, there are certain types of hotels built within palaces, forts and some of hotels with in huge ships.

Heritage hotels: The ancient historical places, forts and havelies have now been converted into luxury hotels, which are also referred to as 'heritage hotels'. This process of conversion in india started as early as 1950. The heritage hotels are said to be old palaces of the kings and monarchs of ancient India. It is said that the heritage hotels were started as movement to not enrich the tourist of India's past glory but also to make the tourist take back with them the Indian history. The present data on the hotel industry in India states that the heritage hotels have grown over the years and they are around 200 in number.

Palace on wheels: A unique finding of Indian tourism to attract tourist — both the international and national is through luxury tourist train called the 'palace on wheels'. The palace on wheels has graced the Rajasthan tourism and the Indian railways. Its inaugaural operation started October 1982. Rated as one of the best ten luxury railway journey, in the world.

The fully air conditioned train with class comforts and personalized service has been a favourite with tourists from the world over and a major foreign exchange earner for the country. The luxury train Comprises fourteen deluxe saloons. Each saloon is a combination of four twin bedded chambers with channel music, intercom, attached toilets with wall to wall carpeting. It also offers a multi cuisine menu. The train has a capacity of 104 berths. It offers a heart-vending trip to the splendid fort and palaces of Rajasthan in just seven days.

The journey to the hinter land of the desert starts every Wednesday at 18.00 hours and ends the following Wednesday at 7.30 hours. The enchanting journey which lasts for seven days takes the tourist to Jaipur (known for its splendid palaces also called the pink city), Chittaurgarh, Udaipur, Jaisalmer, Jodhpur, Bikaner, Fatehpur Sikri, Red fort, and the Taj mahal.

1.5. SIGNIFICANCE OF THE HOTEL INDUSTRY

The growth of any sector involves not only its own growth and establishment, but the significant benefits it provides to the economy as a whole. The hotel industry in that way has provided manifold benefits to the economy. They include:

Hotel industry and the Economy: The contribution of any sector to the economic system is measured by the value of its output or 'value added'. Value added gives measure of the contribution made by the factors of production employed in the sector which is a measure of value produced with in the sector. It represents the contribution to gross domestic product*. In the context of the

* refer appendix.

hotel industry also it is seen that each unit of the demand for hotel's product generates within the industry a high percentage of value added, each unit of value addition produced by this industry demands a higher input of labour and raw materials.

Inter-linkages: In any economy, no industry has operated in isolation. A demand for hotel services generates activity in a number of industries and ancillary concerns. Its implication is that the economic effect of the demand for hotel services are not confined to the hotel industry itself but are spread throughout the economy. The effects of the demand for hotel products in the economy can be classified into:

1. **Direct effect:** It relates to those activities related directly to the industry.
2. **Indirect effect:** It relates to activity of ancillary units, which supply ancillary products to the main hotel.
3. **Induced effect:** Relates the secondary activities. The income generated through factor payments should either be saved, taxed, or spent on importables. If this does not occur, it is in turn spent on the domestic products and thereby creates an induced effect.

The real significance of hotel industry however, is thought, to lie not so much in the overall size of its effect and contribution to the general economic activity of a back economy, and also in three specific aspects in which it plays a crucial role.

Employment: Hotel industry creates manifold employment opportunities to skilled and semi-skilled personnel.

Regional economic activity: though as a service industry, it is profit oriented, it provides a sizeable revenue to the government. The growth of hoteliering and related activities has reached out many sectors of the economy. The hotel industry in India has been revolutionized through the advent of automobile and easy transportation facilities. The traveller in need of accommodation is longer tied to the hotels in the vicinity of the railways stations or bus terminals but can go from point to point in search of accommodation which serves his tastes as well his financial status. This has led to competition no longer confined to a number of hotels located in the center of the town, but it has extended to various class of establishments scattered throughout the town and even to other remote areas.

In view of the immense tourist potential of the state, the hotel industry has a significant role to play not only in the national economy and Indian tourism, but also occupies a pivotal position in gearing the parameters of its backward economy, enriching the regional economy of the state, where the incidence of poverty, unemployment and inequality is predominant.

Balance of payment: Indian tourism potentials are exquisite and immense. The scope for earning foreign exchanges from tourism and income generation is manifold. The flow of foreign tourist helps in generating a lot of foreign, exchange which helps in bringing down the deficit in the balance of payments.

Thus the hotel industry plays an important role in developing the economy.

1.6. TOURISM

Tourism is an ever expanding smokeless service industry with latent vast growth potential and has therefore become one of the pivotal concerns of not only the nations but also of international community as a whole. Today tourism and holiday culture on global as well as national level is an exhibition and description of peace and prosperity, higher standard of living and fast emerging concept of paid holiday. Tourism owes its outset to the onset of the transport revolution. The process of tourism incorporates man, space and time as its principal component. Tourism has also emerged as a most instrumental phenomena in the economic and social development of society. Tourism sector's contribution to the GNP and employment generation at the global as well as national level is a testimony in itself that has genuinely led it to gain increasingly important place in the worldwide academic and business like agenda.

Tourism, has an history dating back to 1811. Tourism as a concept can be viewed from different perspectives. It is an activity in which people are engaged in travel away from primarily for business or pleasure. It is a business providing goods and services to travellers involving any expenditure incurred by or for a visitor for his/her trip. Tourism is an overarching business comprising hundreds of component businesses, some huge but mostly small businesses, including airlines, cruise lines, railroads, rental car agencies, restaurants, travel marketers, lodging, and others. There are also travel reception services, commercial campgrounds and parts of retail shops, food stores and gas stations. Many other businesses share in tourism. Restaurants are an example. Like dozens of other business, they serve the traveller with the basic essential like food and accommodation.

Though tourism as an industry is made up of hundreds of businesses, integration and concentration is taking place in some via ownership, cross-ownership, marketing and franchising. Several airlines own all or part of tour companies in Europe. Some airlines are cross owned and a number of airlines own part or all of hotel chains. British Airways is an example of an airline engaged in several tourism ventures. Hotels like the Penta Hotel, Sun resorts in Mauritius and a few others are tour operators and travel agents.

Tourism became a significant international item of trade in parts of Europe as early as the 1900s. Before World War I, Switzerland was receiving as many as half million visitors a year. International travel statistics were collected on a world wide basis in 1947 which led to its publication. In 1961 the OECD established a committee for coordinating studies, organizing meeting of member countries to improve statistical methods of monetary exchange and accounting of the tourism sector. Thus Tourism may be viewed as an economic activity and thus an industry. Tourism has been identified as one of the fastest growing industries in the world. It has grown from the pursuits of a privileged few to a mass movement of people with an urge to discover the unknown to explore new and strange places to seek changes in environment and to undergo new experiences.

A foreign tourist must spend a minimum of 24 hours and a maximum of six months in a country other than his own, living in hotels or other commercial accommodations where he pays in his own currency. A foreigner who comes and works in a country to make a living or to study in its universities is not counted as tourist. This definition has also been developed by the World Tourism Organisation and accepted by about 110 member countries.

The united nations defines a tourist is a temporary visitor to a country other than the one in which he usually resides for any reason other than following an occupation remunerated with the country visited. It further elaborated that the temporary period should not be less than 24 hours.

1.7. FORMS OF TOURISM

Tourism has been divided into different forms on the basis of length of stay, type of transport used, price paid in a group. They are:

Domestic tourist: A domestic tourist is one who travels more than 50 miles away from home and spends at least a night in a hotel or some place where he has to pay. Domestic tourism does not involve use of foreign currency nor causes any balance of payment problem.

International tourism: When people travel to a country other than their own with different economic and political system, the movement becomes international tourism. It involves preparation of several documents, passport, visa etc., to cross the national boundaries of foreign country. It also involves conversion of one's own currency to the currency of the country where one is traveling. It is also likely that the visitor may face the problem of foreign language. The size of a country determines the extent of international tourism. USA for instance is a very large country and has many domestic tourist attractions.

Long haul tourism: Long haul tourism comprises journeys exceeding 5000 kms. If the journey is below that, it is considered as short haul tourism. It is said that the potential tourist markets of India are long haul in nature.

1.8. OBJECTIVES OF TOURISM

Tourism enterprise and entrepreneurs pursue many goals they include:

Profit maximization: Since tourism industry functions as any other industry, its main objective is also to make profits. The development of various tourist interest helps in bringing vast number of tourist who inturn help in improving the profit of the industry.

Sales maximisation : It is a related but more a simplistic goal, in which the gross revenues are maximized. Due to the growth of the tourism industry the various sub-ordinnate industries like that of the hotel industry, trave! agents, transport are making profits by offering their services for a price. It can also be seen that the places of tourist interest charge the visitors with a very small fee like that of entry fee. This income though may be very minimal, but still acts as a profit for the industry.

Out put maxismisation : This can take the form of increasing the facilities offered by the tourism industry, which inturn helps in increasing its revenue.

Empire building : Prestige enhancement has become the paramount goal of the tourism industry. It is seen that it seeks neither maximum profit, sales, output, market share nor prestige—but rather it is mix of business and leisure that produces the greatest overall happiness in their life. They infact combine hobby with a job or the potential to enjoy part time or seasonal employment while having sufficient leisure and income to pursue other interests.

1.9. SIGNIFICANCE OF TOURISM

Tourism is recognized as an industry that generates a number of social and economic benefits. It promotes national integration and international understanding, creates employment opportunities and augments foreign exchange earnings. It also gives support to local handicrafts and cultural activities. R.W. Mc intosh in his article, 'some tourism economics' reveals the economic advantage from tourism. According to him, "tourism may prove to be a valuable source of foreign exchange, within a country, it may have a marked effect on the distribution effect on the distribution of incomes between different regions, acting as an injection of spending power to underdeveloped areas."

Tourism, today, plays an important role in the economy of most countries of the world and India is no exception. Though India was a late starter in this field, its importance was not realized till the seventies. International tourism in India has grown substantially over the last three decades. The growth in foreign tourist arrivals accelerated and the country received million of tourists. India's share in the world tourist market is about 0.30 per cent. Foreign exchange earnings from tourism is on the increase continuously. Tourism now has been given the status of an 'export industry' by the ministry of tourism and the planning commission.

The importance of tourism as an important instrument for economic development and employment generation, particularly in remote and backward areas, has now been well recognized all over the world. It is an important activity for cultural interaction, social upliftment and environment conservation.

(1) Social Benefits

National integration : The Indian country is known for its diverse culture. People with varied languages, religions, caste and creed have lived in India over many centuries. The social activities, the religious festivals which these people celebrate though unique and different in every way brings out the harmony of the people living in the region.

Architectural monuments: Tourist of any region — whether they are domestic tourist or foreigners are attracted to the art and architecture of the country. Indian architecture is known for its splendour-whether one speaks of the beautiful palaces or the memorial monuments of the north or the cave temples of central India, or the stone temples of the south, speak of the rich sculptural heritage. A vast number of tourist visit these places, hence it becomes essential to preserve this rich heritage.

Arts and crafts and Culture: India is a country known for its diverse art and crafts, the entire expanse of the region have their own unique art and craft forms which pose great attraction to the tourist, especially foreigners.

International understanding: Tourisms helps in understanding the life styles of people. At times it also play a role in bringing people of diverse culture together thereby promoting peace.

(2) Economic Benefits

Direct employment: Tourism is a service based industry and such has been partly responsible for the service sector growth. In developing countries, the service sector is responsible for 40% of the GDP, while in developing economies, it is responsible for more than 65 per cent GDP. In India tourism has created direct employment for 12 million people. It generates large scale employment in remote and backward areas. Tourism as a source of employment is particularly important for areas with limited alternative sources of employment. It creates 89 per cent jobs in the hotel and restaurant sector like providing jobs to hoteliers, travel agents, taxi drivers, craftsmen, transporters, airlines, tourist guides and shoe makers. It offers enormous potential for the economic utilization of natural attractions like mountains, beaches, rivers etc. The share of tourism in the tøtal employment is about 3.2 per cent. It is thus clear that tourism can play a major role in promoting large scale employment opportunities.

Self employment: The rich heritage of handicrafts and handloom are manufactured by small craftsmen in their houses, these craft forms are very exquisite in nature. Tourist have a special attraction for these handicrafts. This inturn helps the small craftsmen a market for their goods.

Women labour: Tourism helps in generating women employment, thereby uplifting the weaker sections.

(3) Environmental impacts

The environment, whether it natural or man made is the most fundamental ingredient of the tourism product. As soon as tourism activity takes place, the environment is inevitably changes or modified to facilitate tourism. Infact tourism at times supports conservation. This will indirectly help in increasing the income of local inhabitants, business firms and the local authority may be channeled through taxes in to conservation work.

The environmental impacts associated with tourism development can also be considered in terms of their direct and indirect effects. The impacts can be positive or negative. It is not possible to develop tourism without incurring environmental impacts, but it is possible with correct planning to manage tourism development in order to minimize the negative impacts, while encouraging the positive impacts. For instance, if tourism is misutilised it destroys the culture and peace of the people of the host country.

(4) Multiplier effect

It is seen that tourism — both domestic and international, has a multiplier effect which appears to be large than any other industry. The tourism helps the économy of a country by a number of multiples of the tourists original dollar. In simple terms the multiplier means that every unit of tourist expenditure goes through various rounds of income creation and expenditure before it loses its effect. For example the money spent by the tourist during his stay in the hotel on various services obtained like food and beverage, accommodation, transportation etc., becomes an income to the hotel staff. They in turn would spend on goods of their own liking, this forms the second cycle of expenditure, which in turn becomes the income of the sellers of these goods.

Thus the money spent by the tourist percolates through the numerous segments of the economy. It is thus seen the money spent on a particular sector. In the example the income generated by the hotel industry does not remain ideal with the hotelier, instead it moves around within the economy acting as an income for one and expenditure for another. Similarly, if the propensity to save in a community is fairly high the number of rounds of expenditure will be correspondingly reduced. The imports for hotels constitute only six or seven per cent of the total cost. But there are other items of foreign currency expenditure such as purchase of aircraft, equipment of airports, oil imports, part of which can be attributed to tourism. All these plus expenditure publicity and promotion may add up to about 12 per cent leakage of receipts from tourism.

(5) Business

Tourism is source of income to hundreds of millions of individuals world-wide. Workers and employers alike can benefit from tourism in that — (1) it improves the efficiency of business structures and administrative arrangements. (2) improves the strategies for coping with the risk and uncertainity inherent in the industry. (3) offers a firmer basis for profitable marketing. (4) offers improvements in the terms and conditions of employment. (5) promotes pride, professional development and rewarding careers in the industry.

National integration : Tourism contributes to national integration .Over 100 million tourists visiting different parts of the country every year return with a better understanding of the people living in the different regions of the country and the cultural diversity of the country.

1.10. GROWTH OF TOURISM

There exist immense tourist attractions in India, both natural and man made which attract foreign tourist to a great extent. Tourism has a distinct feature over other industries, in that there are no tendencies to consume or rate the scarce resources of the country. The basic tourist items being that of monuments, temples beaches, performing arts and wild life. These natural and to some extent man made monuments, and natural beauty of the greenery attract millions of foreign tourist.

Foreign tourist arrivals between 1950-1991 : International tourism in India has grown steadily since 1950, as also the revenue from international tourism. Revenue from tourism means a lot to the host country as it is contributed by foreign tourist in dollars or other hard currency which the host country can use for its economic development. The table below explains the flow of foreign tourist over a period of fifty years and the earnings made thereon.

Year	*international tourist Arrivals (thousands) (India)*	*international tourist receipts million of U.S Dollars*
1950	25,262	2,100
1960	69,296	6,867
1965	112,729	10,073
1970	159,690	17,900
1975	214,357	40,702
1980	284,840	102,363
1985	325,725	108,091
1990	429,000	249,000
1991	450,000	278,000

The above table indicates that the foreign tourist arrivals over a period of fifty years have been continuously increasing. The manifold increase in the foreign tourist speaks of the Indian tourism growth. The revenue from international tourist receipts have also steadily grown over the years. The growth of tourism has grown steadily over the years. An analysis of tourist arrivals shows that there has been an increasing trend in the number of tourist that has visited India. The international tourist arrivals was only 25,262 in 1960. It increased to 69,296, which was more than twice the number of the 1950's. This trend has seen to increase over the years. In 1990 the tourist arrivals amounted to a whopping 450,000 thousand but a reverse happened in 1991 where the foreign tourist arrivals amounted to only 450,000.

1. Foreign Tourist Arrivals between 1991-2001 :

Year	*Numbers (figs in Lakhs)*
1991	16.8
1992	18.7
1993	17.7
1994	18.9
1995	21.2
1996	22.9
1997	23.8
1998	23.6
1999	24.8
2000	26.2
2001	26.8

Tourist arrivals — the growth between 1991-2001

The Indian economy has witnessed a tremendous influx of foreign tourists from times immemorial. The growth of Hindusim, Buddhism, Jainism had led to the growth of foreigners into the country. Who were not only visitors, but who also contributed to a major flow of tourists. The globalisation of the Indian economy led to tremendeous charges. In 1991 the number of tourists stood at 16.8 lakhs. By 1992, this numbers increased by nearly 2 lakhs. But this suddenly declined by 1 lakhs in 1993. The next year only saw the growth of tourists increase by 1.2 lakhs. Though the next few years also witnessed the increase in the numbers of foreign tourists the percentage increase does not show a phenomenal increase.

There can be various factors atributed to a marginal or least increase in the number of tourists to India.

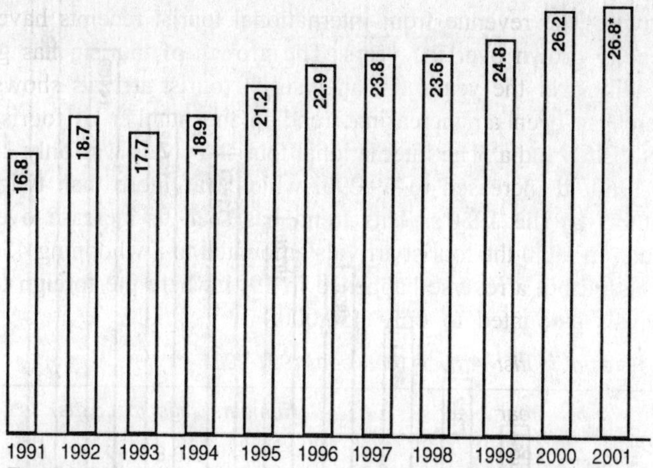

Figures in lakh * Source : Economic Survey 2001-02

- The fears of disease most foreigners consider India to be a poor country with spread of epidemic disceases. This prevents them from visitings these places.
- Communal problems/violence may also hinder the normal activity in a region leading to a fall in tourist visits.
- Natural calamities like flood earthquakes can also effect the movement of tourist.
- Lastly it is seen that since the flow of foreign tourist are minimal. The tourists visiting India have to incure a high cost of transportation on air fares etc. This can also play a role in bring down the no. of foreign tourists.

2. Foreign Exchange Earnings :

Year	*Earnings (crores)*
1991	4111
1992	5887
1993	6466
1994	7282
1995	8633
1996	9920
1997	10726
1998	11951
1999	13042
2000	14409
2001	15364

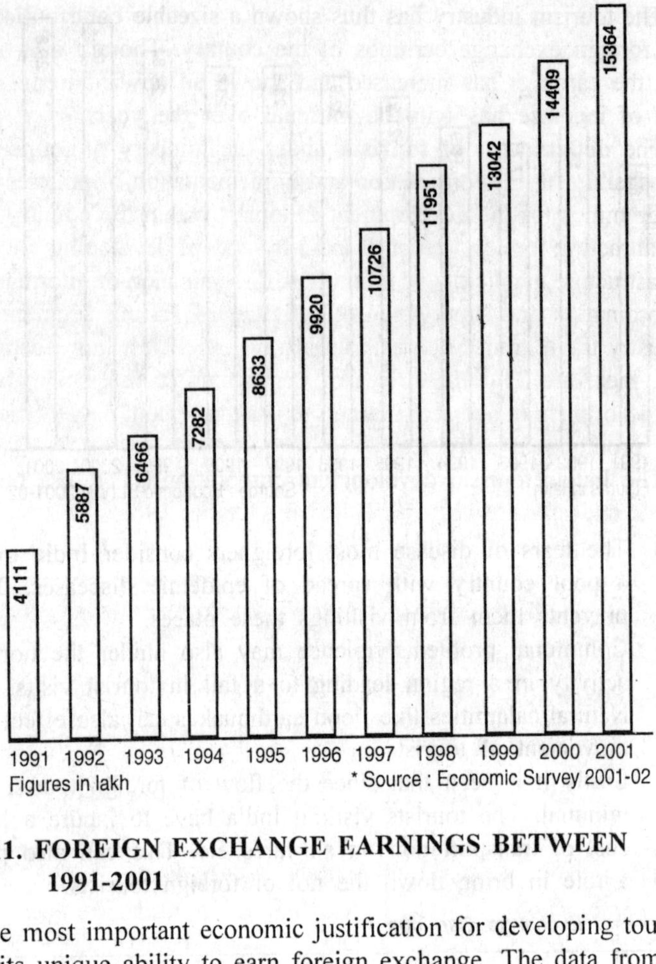

Figures in lakh * Source : Economic Survey 2001-02

1.11. FOREIGN EXCHANGE EARNINGS BETWEEN 1991-2001

The most important economic justification for developing tourism is its unique ability to earn foreign exchange. The data from the table on foreign exchange earnings shows that there has been a higher growth in the last ten decades. In 1991, the exchange earnings amounted to Rs. 4111 crores it gradually increased by roughly 2000 crores in the following years. In 1993 to tourist earnings stood at 6466 crores. The next 3 years i.e., 1993 to 1996 saw a minimal increase in the exchange earnings. In 1998, the earnings had a quantum jump and stood at 11.951 crores. The 1999 figures show that the foreign exchange earnings stood at Rs. 13042 crores in 2000 it increased by a 1500 crores. The final annual figures of 2001. Stood at 15,364 crores.

The tourism industry has thus shown a sizeable contribution to the foreign exchange earnings of the country. Though it is seen that the earnings has increased and shown an upward trend. The rate of increase has only be minimal over the years.

The **department of tourism** under the ministry of tourism is responsible for the formulation and implementation of policies and programmes for the development of tourist within the country and for attracting foreign tourist to India by way of developing tourism infrastructure, publicity and promotion, dissemination of information, co-ordination and supervision of activities of various segments of industry travel trade such as hotels, travel agencies, tour operators etc., there are 21 field offices of department of tourism in India and 18 of them in overseas markets to undertake both developmental and promotional activities.

The Indian tourism development corporation (ITDC), a public sector undertaking was established in October 1966, the activities of the corporation include:

Construction, management and marketing of hotels, restaurants, travellers lodge for tourist at various places in the country.

- Provision of tourist transport facilities.
- Production, distribution and sale of tourist publicity materials.
- Provision of entertainment facilities such as light and sound shows.
- Provision of consultancy-cum-managerial service in India and abroad.

The Indian Institute of Tourism and Travel Management is an autonomous body set up to provide education in tourism and travel management. The institute also organizes executive development programmes, seminars and workshops relating to tourism and travel management. The department of tourism has accorded high priority to the development of manpower to meet the growing needs of hotels, restaurants and other tourism industries. 30 institutes of hotel management and catering technology and 13 food crafts institutes have been set up in the country. These institutes conduct diploma courses in the fields of Hotel Management and catering technology and applied nutrition and craft courses in food and beverage services.

In order to encourage adventure tourism, the department of

Tourism has set up a National institute of Water Sports (NIWS) at Goa and institute of skiing and Mountaineering (IISM) at Gulmarg. The IISM conducts courses at Auli, Patnitop, Gulmarg, and Kulu. These institutes act as the nodal centers for adventure and sports oriented tourism activities in the country.

The hotel sector forms one of the most important segments of the tourism industry with high potential for employment generation and foreign exchange earnings. To give impetus to this sector, the government provides tax benefits and other incentives. The industrial policy has now placed hotels and tourism related activities as a priority industry. Foreign investment and collaborations are now facilitated under the new economic policy. Up to 51 per cent foreign equity is now granted automatically. Non-resident Indians are allowed cent per cent investment.

The Department of Tourism classifies functioning hotels under the 'star system' into various categories from one to five-star deluxe. The newly introduced category is the 'heritage hotels'. The department reclassifies these hotels after every three years to ensure that they maintain the requisite standards. A new classification standard of heritage hotels has been introduced to cover functioning hotels in palaces.

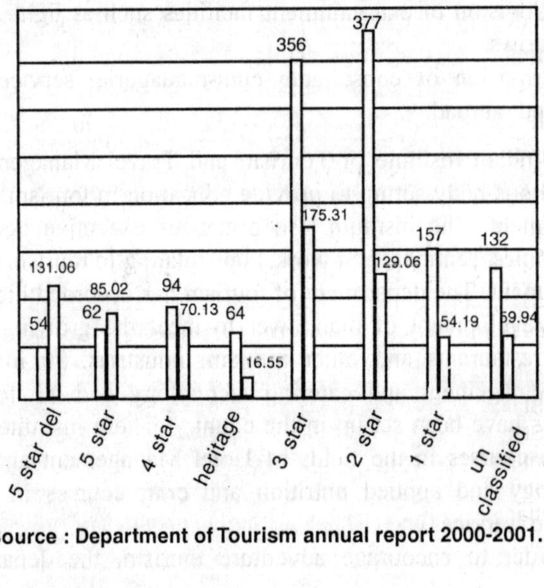

Source : Department of Tourism annual report 2000-2001.

1.12. THE TYPES OF HOTELS

The hotels in India are basically classified on the basis of the luxury and facilities which they provide. It is seen that the number of star hotels run by the private group as well as the govt. has increased rapidly over the years. The figures published by department of tourism 2000-2001 reveals growth of the hotels has been tremendous over the years.

Though the growth of star hotels like the five star delux, five star and three star have been minimal it is seen that the accomodiation (in relation to rooms) offered by them have been consistent with that of the three star hotels. It shows how the five star hotels, though their number being less have increased their accomodation facilities.

The number of three star hotels has also been rapid. Their numbers stood at 356 and with a capacity of 17350 rooms. Though the 3 star hotels change more or less a piece which are changed by the five star hotels. They only differ in the type of accomodation and facility they offer to their customers.

The heritage group is another group of hotels these are palaces converted to hotels with very good luxury facilities provided in them.

The decline of the monarchy has led to the conversion of the magnificant palaces into hotels. The heritage hotels are 164 in number it is interesting to note here that though their number is sizeable amounting to 164 of the rooms in these hotels is comparatively low.

The other categories of hotels namely the ones like the 2 star. One star and the unclassified are found to have a higher numbers. This is because of the usage of these hotel accomodation by a bigger crowd.

Types	*No. of Hotels*	*No. of rooms*
5 Star delux	54	13106
5 Star	62	8502
4 Star	94	70113
Heritage	164	1655
3 star	356	17531
2 star	377	12936
1 star	157	5419
un classified	132	5994

In order to provide facilities and to support the increasing flow of tourist, the Paying Guest Accomodation Scheme has been introduced in major tourist centers. This scheme is open to the house owners having lettable rooms of requisite standard. This scheme is been constituted in different regions. There are around 280 tour operators, 197 travels agents and 150 transport operators. With the liberalization process after 1991, more preference is given to foreign tourist. The system of granting clearances has been liberalized to attract the tourist. Various tourist schemes have made operational like the one of the Rajasthan tourism, which has introduced the 'Palace on wheels', a luxury train for tourist. The 'Orient Express' has been introduced in the Gujarat Sector.

1.13. CONSTRAINTS OF TOURISM

Tourism by nature is international. Consequently the industry is extremely sensitive to fluctuations in the international economy. At times it is seen that the exchange rates of currency affects the potential prospects of the tourism programme it self. The fall off in travel by the U.S citizens following the devaluation of the dollar in the early 1970's can be example to quote.

- Tourism businesses are especially vulnerable to exogenous forces. Political instability or terrorism will harm businesses in one country by diverting tourists to other destinations, in turn benefiting business in those nations that tourist visit.. Example, the bombings of twin towers of the world trade organization, in USA in September 2001, suddenly saw a fall in the business of aircrafts. This was because of the fall in the demand for the service of the different airlines. Though Jammu and Kashmir in India is considered to be the most beautiful state to attract foreign tourist in large numbers, it is said that of late the tourist inflow has drastically fallen due to the growing terrorism and unrest in the region. Disease, natural disasters, communal violence, unfavourable changes in the currency exchange, new tax rates, or alteration in border crossing formalities can quickly and dramatically alter the tourists visits. However the tourism operators through their personal experience can cope with these problems. Their coping mechanisms however can be improved if they have access to professional development courses, professional literature or consultants.

- A major constraint in the growth of tourism in India is the lack of adequate infrastructural facilities, especially air transport, the first major step would be to increase the use of private airways to facilitate movement of tourists within and outside the country. This would also prevent undue waste of time at airports on account of long delay in flights arrivals and departures. It is also hoped that the "open sky" policy will go a long way in increasing tourist traffic in India.
- Poor facilities have also affected tourism. It is seen that 98 per cent of tourists arrivals in India are by air. The ministry of civil aviation and the interanational airports authority must help to improve facilities for passengers amenities at international terminal over crowding at airports, inadequate road and rail access to airports.

Large private investment has to be mobilised to achieve significant developments in tourism. The government has a role to play to facilitiate and also act path-setters by putting up lead projects and basic facilities like information centres, low priced accomodation units etc., apart from all necessary support services to initiate the process of development with a view to avoiding over exploitation and achieving sustainable growth in tourism. It is seen that since most of the tourist attraction and delivery system as with in the purview of state govts. a large part of the central govt. investment for the improvement and creation of tourist facilitites is channelised through the state governments on a cost sharing basis.

1.14. TOURISM POLICY

The Department of tourism is a nodal agency for the formulation of national policies and programmes and for the co-ordination of activities of various central govt. agencies, state govt. and the private sector for the development of tourism in the country. The office provides executive directions for the implementation of various policies and programmes. The department has a field formation of 18 offices aboraod and 21 offices within the country.

The overseas offices are primarily responsible for tourism

promotion and marketing in their respective areas and field offices. The Department is a Nodal agency for the development of tourism in the country. It plays an important role in co-ordinating and supplementry the efforts of the state/U.T. govt. catalising private investment, strengthening promotional and marketing efforts and in providing trained manpower resources. The functions of the department consists mainly of the following:

- policy formulation and planning
- coordination
- infrastructure and product and develt
- regulation
- human resource development
- publicity marketing and facilitation
- research analysis monitoring and evaluation
- legislation and parliament work.

Policy

The department has the responsibility of formulating national level policies and programmes for the development of tourism on sustainable basis. Recognising its importance as an instrument for economic development, a comprehensive tourism policy highlighting the objectives of tourism development in the country was promulgated by the govt. during 1982. It specified the responsibility for tourism development as a common endeavour of all the agencies vitally concerned with tourism at central and state levels, including public and private sector times air, railways and road transport systems.

The plan proposed to achieve intensive development of selected circuits to dispel the tendency of concentration in a few urban centres encourage the diversification of tourist attractions and opening up economically backward areas which hold many tourist attractions. Man power development and treasing were also given due weightage to ensure efficient services and effective management of tourist facilities. In 1991 tourism was also declared as priority sector for foreign investment.

Tourism is one of the world's biggest businesses with a turnover as large of that of the oil industry. Though travel has a long history modern tourism only started in the eighteen century with the advent various findings in science and technology. It is therefore a young industry, yet it is the fastest growing in the world. Tourism is labour intensive and creates many jobs — for hoteliers, transport agents, various means of transport. It generates economic activity in the host cities, states and countries. It is considered an major export earner — in invisible exports which earns foreign exchange with exporting tangible goods. It is also called a smokeless industry as no factories are needed to make goods for exports.

2
Consumption

2.1. UTILITY ANALYSIS OF DEMAND

When a consumer demands a commodity, he expects the commodity to give in satisfaction. When a consumer buys a commodity, his demand depends on factors like the price, his income and above all his preference for the commodity. Utility plays a important role when the consumer buys his commodity. Economists have thus used various theories to explain the concept of utility. The utility analysis of demand is broadly divided in to two methods.

1. Marshallian method known as Cardinal Utility Approach.
2. Hicksian method or Indifference Curve Method.

2.2. CONCEPTS RELATED TO THE TWO APPROACHES

Utility: The want satisfying power of the commodity is known as utility. When a consumer buys a commodity, he obtains a certain level of satisfaction. This satisfying power is what is termed as utility.

Total utility: The total satisfaction derived by the consumer when he consumes a certain amount of the commodity is termed as total utility. For example if the consumer consumes 10 slices of bread and obtains 25 units of utility. The 25 units of satisfaction is known as total utility. In mathematical terms, the total utility is a direct function of the number of units of a commodity under consideration.

To put it symbolically TUx = F(Qx).

Average utility: It is also known as the per unit amount of utility derived. The total utility divided by the number of units is termed as average utility. For instance if the consumer buys a dozen mangoes and obtains 150 units of satisfaction. His average utility is 150/12, his average utility becomes 15 units.

Marginal utility: Additional utility derived out of an additional unit consumed is termed as marginal utility. Marginal utility analysis has been developed to occupy an important place in economic theory. According to Professor Boulding "marginal utility of any quantity of commodity is the increase in the total utility which results from a units increase in consumption". Thus the marginal utility may be measured as the difference between the utility of the total units of stock of consumption of a given commodity minus that of consuming one unit less in the stock considered. Thus, $Mu_n = Tu_n - Tu_{n-1}$.

Units of x	*Total utility*	*Marginal utility*
1	10	-
2	20	10
3	30	10

In the above imaginary schedule, total utility obtained by consuming the one unit of the commodity is 10 units. And consuming the second unit the total utility is 20 units. The marginal utility is obtained by subtracting the total utility 20 by its preceding value which is 10 units. Thus the marginal utility obtained by consuming the additional one unit is 10 units.

2.3. CARDINAL UTILITY APPROACH

According to the cardinal analysis, the utility is measured is terms of 'utils' or units. According to Marshall, utility of a commodity is quantifiable, he assumed that if a consumer brought a loaf of bread, it gave 15 units of satisfaction. Thus when satisfaction is measured in mathematical terms it is referred to as cardinal utility. There are two laws which are related to the cardinal principle:

1. The law of Diminishing Marginal utility.
2. The law of equi-marginal utility.

The Law of Diminishing Marginal Utility

The principle behind the law of diminishing marginal utility is that, as an individual consumer consumes more and more of a commodity, he desire for the commodity gradually decreases and he consumes less of that commodity, as he is indifferent to it. This tendency of the consumer is reflected in every commodity the consumer consumes.

The law states that "Other things being equal, as the quantity of commodity consumed or acquired by the consumer increases, the marginal utility of the commodity tends to diminish". As a person purchases more and more units of a commodity, its marginal utility decreases. Boulding defines it as "When a consumer increases the consumption of any one commodity, keeping constant the consumption of all other commodities, the marginal utility of the variable commodity must eventually decline". Marshall defines it as, "The additional benefit which a person derives from a given increase of his stock of a thing diminishes with every increase in the stock that he already has". For instance if person Z is consuming bread. The first slice of bread gives him 30 units of utility. The second one gives 25 units of utility, the third one 16 units of utility. The fourth one gives him 12 units of utility. And 5th slice gives him only 5 units of utility. Thus it is seen from the above example, that as the individual consumes more and more of a commodity his satisfaction gradually diminishes.

Utility Schedule

Units of commodity	*Total Utility*	*Marginal Utility*
1	20	20
2	37	7
3	49	12
4	58	9
5	64	6
6	64	0
7	62	–2

The law of diminishing marginal utility can be explained through a schedule. From the schedule, it is seen that as the consumer goes on consuming more and more of units his additional satisfaction gradually diminishes. When the consumer consumes the first unit, his total utility and marginal utility remain at 20 units. When he consumes the second unit, his total utility increases to 37 units, marginal utility decreases to 17 units, and when he consumes the third unit, his marginal further more decreases to 12 units. As the consumer goes on buying more and more of the commodity, his additional or marginal utility gradually diminishes, and when he consumes the sixth unit of the commodity, his marginal utility becomes zero. Though the total utility seems to increase, it increases at a diminishing rate. If the consumer continues to consume his marginal utility becomes negative as seen in the schedule. When he consumes the seventh unit, he obtains a negative marginal utility of –2 units.

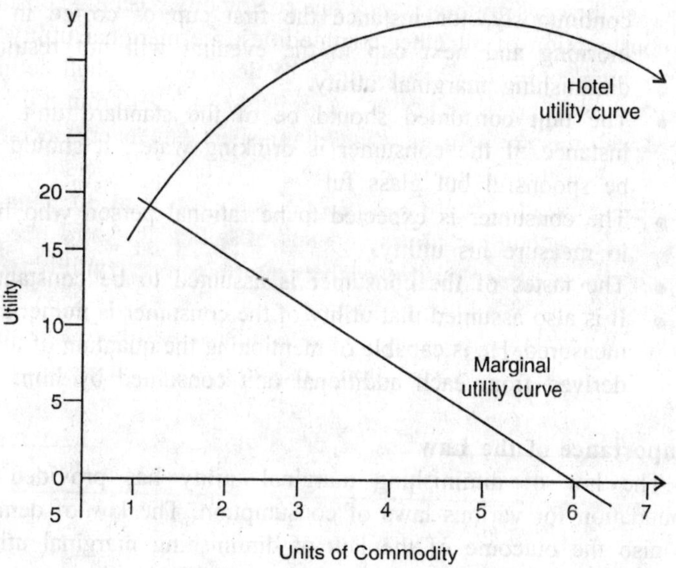

The law of diminishing marginal utility can also be explained through a figure. On the Y axis utility of the units is measured. And on the X axis units of the commodity is measured. With the data available from the schedule, the total utility and marginal utility at various levels of consumption are pointed. As shown in the figure, the total utility curve ascends, reaches the maximum point and then begins to decline. Marginal utility declines gradually reaches a zero level and then a negative level. The point where the marginal utility curve touches the X axis is known as the point of satiety, where the total utility is at its maximum. After this point even if the consumer desires to buy the commodity he will be only dissatisfied with the commodity.

Assumptions

- The successive units of the commodities consumed should be identical and homogenous in all respects with out any difference, or the consumer would obtain more satisfaction by consuming the additional commodity than get less satisfied.
- The consumption process should be continuous, in order to measure its utility. Units of the commodity should be used continuously, for instance the first cup of coffee in the morning and next cup in the evening will not result in diminishing marginal utility.
- The unit consumed should be of the standard unit. For instance, if the consumer is drinking water, it should not be spoonsful but glass ful .
- The consumer is expected to be rational person who likes to measure his utility.
- The tastes of the consumer is assumed to be constant.
- It is also assumed that utility of the consumer is numerically measured. He is capable of mentioning the quantum of utility derived from each additional unit consumed by him.

Importance of the Law

The law of diminishing marginal utility has provided the foundation for various laws of consumption. The law of demand is also the outcome of the law of diminishing marginal utility. According to the law of demand, large quantities are purchased at less price and vice versa. This is because when more units are purchased, its marginal utility to the consumer becomes less and less and so he gives lesser importance to additional units of the commodity and thus buy additional units only at a lower price.

A rational consumer seeks to maximize his level of satisfaction from the commodities he buys. When he is confronted with combination of many goods and alternatives. He would rank them according to the different levels of satisfaction in order to decide. Such a conceptual ordering of different goods and their combinations in a set order of preferences is termed as the scale of preferences. Here the economists wanted to find whether a particular combination of goods gave utility to the consumer as another combination of goods. It is thus seen that the concept of scale of preference does not attempt to measure utility at all. It is only a device by which the utilities of commodities are compared and chosen. The scale of preference is given a practical shape through the indifference curve technique. The law also explains the paradox of value-in-use and value-in-exchange. Diamonds have great value in exchange as they are scarce in supply and priced high, where as water is in abundant supply and its marginal utility is very low. Therefore it commands less though its utility is high. Thus water has great value in use but no value in exchange. Diamonds have great value in exchange, though they are less useful than water.

2. LAW OF EQUI-MARGINAL UTILITY

A consumer obtains satisfaction when he is at the equilibrium. This is a point of satiety. As he gets maximum satisfaction he will not change his outlay. The consumer will allocate his resources on various items of expenditure in such way as to secure the maximum satisfaction and thereby attain equilibrium. The principle of consumer's equilibirium is explained through the law of maximum satisfaction. This law is referred to as the law of equi-marginal utility or the law of consumer's demand.

One Commodity Principle

The law states that 'Other things being equal, a consumer's gets maximum total utility from spending his given income, when he allocates his expenditure to the purchase of different goods in such a way that the marginal utilities derived from the last unit of money spent on each item of expenditure tends to be equal'. It is said that the consumer gets maximum satisfaction when he obtains maximum additional satisfaction from the last unit consumed. The consumer being rational will not pay more for a commodity and obtain less satisfaction. If the marginal utility is more, he will buy the commodity as he stands, to gain by getting more satisfaction while spending. He will stop buying just when the marginal utility is equal to price. The law can be illustrated through a figure.

In the figure below quantity is measured on the X axis, whereas on the Y axis the Price and Marginal utility is drawn. The down ward sloping curve shows that as the consumer purchases more and more the utility for each unit is declining. At the market price OP, the consumer goes on purchasing as the utility derived from each unit is larger than the price OP paid. When the consumer is purchasing 5th unit of the commodity the marginal utility is BM and the price is EM, the utility obtained is BE. At this point the consumer does not get any extra benefit or satisfaction. The

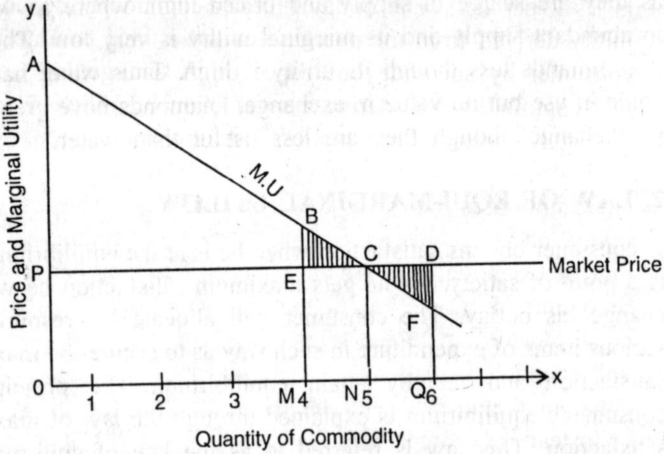

utility derived just equals the price paid. If he purchases the 7th unit the utility he gets is FQ which is lesser than the price paid DQ which is equal to OP. A consumer being rational will not be prepared to pay more and get less utility. Hence he will stop at ON units. Where he gets maximum satisfaction.

Two Commodity Principle

According to Alfred Marshall, "If a person has a thing which can put to several uses, he will distribute it among those uses in such a way that it has the same marginal utility, for if it had a greater marginal utility in one use than in another, he would gain by taking away some of it from the second use and applying it to the first". The law of equi-marginal utility can also be stated as follows, 'Maximum satisfaction can be derived out of the expenditure of a given sum, if the utility derived from the last unit of money spent on each object of expenditure is more or less equal'. Thus it can be said that the consumer would spend his money on various commodities till the time the marginal utility derived from the last unit of money spent gives him equal satisfaction, for all the goods bought.

Illustration of the Law

Suppose a consumer has Rs. 18 to spend on three commodities A,B and C. The price is assumed of all the three commodities is Rs 2 per unit. The outlay of each commodity depends on the utility derived from the purchase of these three commodities. The consumer by spending one rupee on A and getting one unit of that commodity will derive a satisfaction or utility ab as seen in the figure. In the consumption of the second unit he derives utility cd and in the third ef which is equal to mn derived in the consumption of fourth unit in commodity B. Thus the marginal utility mn is equal to qr derived from the consumption of second unit of Commodity C. So the marginal utilities derived from the third unit of A and fourth unit of B and second unit of C are equal. According to the figure ef = mn = qr. So, the consumer will spend Rs. 6 on A, Rs. 8 on B and Rs. 4 on C and obtain equal marginal utility for all the three commodities.

Instead of purchasing 3 units of A and 4 units of B, the consumer purchases 4 units of A and three units of B. In that case the fourth unit of A will give the consumer utility xy as shown in the figure, instead of mn derived from the fourth unit of B xy is decisively smaller utility than mn and the consumer loses by spending one rupee more on A instead of on B. In this manner the consumer allocates his income on various commodities so that the marginal utilities are the same in order to maximize his satisfaction. In this case the consumer has substituted the fourth unit of B in the place of fourth unit A in order to maximize his satisfaction. Thus it is seen that the consumer distributes his income in such a way that the marginal utilities of the goods in terms of money is equal to their money prices so as to enable him to derive maximum satisfaction.

Mathematical Illustration

The law of equi-marginal utility states that the consumer will distribute his money income between the two goods X and Y in such a way that the utility derived from the last rupee spent on the each commodity is equal. The consumer obtains equilibrium when

$$\frac{\text{Marginal utility of A}}{\text{Price of A}} = \frac{\text{Marginal utility of B}}{\text{Price of B}} = \frac{\text{Marginal utility of C}}{\text{Price of C}}$$

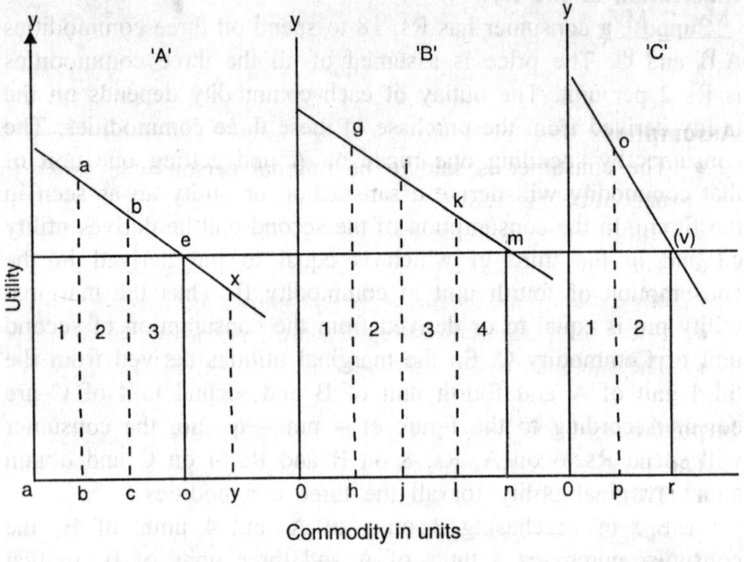

the marginal utility of money expenditure on each commodity is same. Symbolically it may be stated as

$$Mv_e = \frac{Mv_a}{P_a}$$

Where Mv_a is the marginal utility of money expenditure and Mv_a is the marginal utility of commodity A and P_a is the price of commodity A.

The law of equi-marginal utility can therefore be stated thus: the consumer will spend his income on different commodities in such a way that marginal utility of each commodity is proportional to its price. For example the consumer is said to be in equilibrium when marginal utility of commodity A = marginal utility of commodity B.

$$\frac{Mv_a}{P_a} = \frac{Mv_b}{P_b}$$

For instance if $\frac{Mv_a}{P_a}$ is greater than $\frac{Mv_b}{P_b}$ then the consumer will substitute commodity A for commodity B. As a result of which $\frac{Mv_a}{P_a} = \frac{Mv_b}{P_b}$.

Assumptions

- The consumer is said to be rational person who seeks to maximize his utility.
- Utility is measurable in terms of utils.
- The consumer has a given scale of preferences for the goods bought and he also has a perfect knowledge of his utilities.
- Prices of commodities remain unchanged.
- The income of the consumer is assumed to be fixed.

Importance of the Law of Equi-marginal Utility

The law has various practical applications to its credit:

- This principle is made use of in framing the household budget. The income of the household has to be distributed in several ways like of food, shelter, clothing, education of children, recreation etc., thus obtaining welfare of the household is the ultimate objective behind this law.
- In the process of production the producer has to combine the factors in such an economical way for getting maximum returns. He will be constantly substituting one factor for another in a way that gives larger returns. For instance substituting labour for capital. He does this in order to obtain equal marginal returns for all factors.
- In the process of exchange the principle helps in relieving the scarcity of a commodity for consumer to substitute the less scarce good for the more scarce good.

- The government is also guided by this principle government expenditure is guided by the principle which is called maximum social advantage. The principle is nothing but the equi marginality applied in government finance.

Limitation to the Law

- The law is based on unrealistic assumption according to some economists. They are of the view that too many assumptions govern the law like homogeneity, cardinality continuity etc.
- It is also assumed that the measure of utility is unrealistic in nature.
- The law cannot be applied to indivisible goods.

2.4. INDIFFERENCE CURVE ANALYSIS

The cardinal approach was found to be defective in many respects. Hence modern economists have evolved the indifference curve approach, based on the ordinal system. The analysis was formulated by the famous Italian economist Pareto.

The indifference curve analysis is considered to be a geometric device representing all such combinations of two goods yielding equal satisfaction. An indifference curve represents different combinations of two goods that give the same level of satisfaction. It can be defined as the "locus of points representing all the different combinations of two goods (say X and Y) which yield equal level of utility or satisfaction to the consumer." Each point on the indifference curve indicates the same level of satisfaction as any other point on the same curve. Each indifference curve indicates only one level of satisfaction.

Assumptions

1. The consumer is interested in buying only two goods at a point of time. He is aware and has complete knowledge of the prevailing prices in the market.
2. The consumer is assumed to be rational person who with a given income, likes to choose the combination of goods that gives maximum satisfaction.
3. The analysis assumes continuity. Which means that consum-

ers are capable of ordering or ranking all combination of goods to the satisfaction they yield.

4. The consumer has a fixed amount of money which he likes to spend on two goods.
5. The prices of goods are assumed to be constant.
6. The consumer choice is transitive. That is, he is always consistent in his choice, i.e., when he prefers combination a to combination b, b to c, then he must also prefer a to c.
7. He is able to rank his preferences according to the satisfaction which he derives from them.

Indifference schedule

An indifference schedule is a list of alternative combinations in the stock of two goods which yield the same level of satisfaction to the consumer. The various combinations give the consumer equal satisfaction and as such he is indifferent to various combinations. When a consumer sets his preference for different combinations of certain goods under consideration, he will rank them according to the satisfaction he obtains from them. Thus the one yielding less satisfaction he prefers less, and one which gives him more satisfaction he prefers more.

Combination	*Commodity x*	*Commodity y*
A	5	20
B	7	17
C	9	15
D	11	11
E	13	9

From the schedule we can find that in the first combination A Commodity x is demanded less and commodity y is demanded more. And in the second combination B also x is demanded less and commodity y is demanded more. In the combination D both the commodities are demanded equally. And in the combination E more of Commodity x is demanded and less of Commodity y is demanded. It is seen here that all the combinations in the schedule give the consumer equal level of satisfaction.

Indifference Curve

The scale of preference of the consumer can be also explained through a figure. The combinations can be plotted on a graph. The various combinations of the two commodities are plotted and joined to form a curve called the indifference curve. In the figure IC is the indifference curve showing the combinations of the two commodities given in the schedule. All the points on this curve give the consumer the same level satisfaction. Hence an indifference curve represents the loci of various combinations of two goods which give the consumer equal satisfaction.

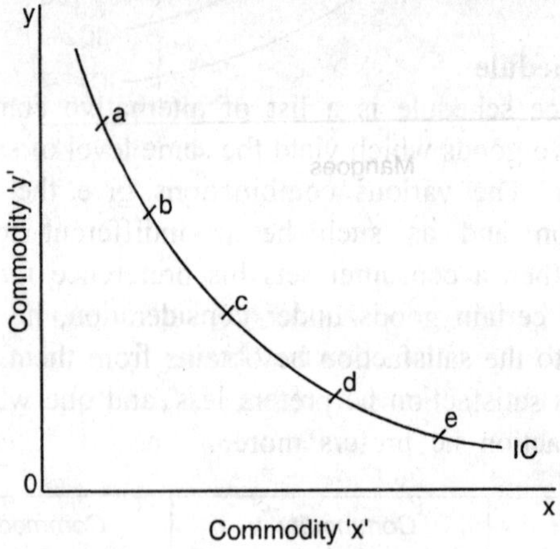

Indifference Map

The indifference curve in the above figure shows the consumer has only one indifference curve in which the various combinations of two commodities give a particular level of satisfaction. A consumer may have any number of such indifference curves for the two commodities showing the different levels of satisfaction. Thus a set of indifference curves, which represent a lower satisfaction and a higher satisfaction is called the indifference map. It can also be said that the indifference map represents a collection of many indifference curves which indicate a certain level of satisfaction.

In the figure units of oranges are measured on the y axis. And on the x axis units of mangoes. Each indifference curve shows different combinations of oranges and mangoes which give the

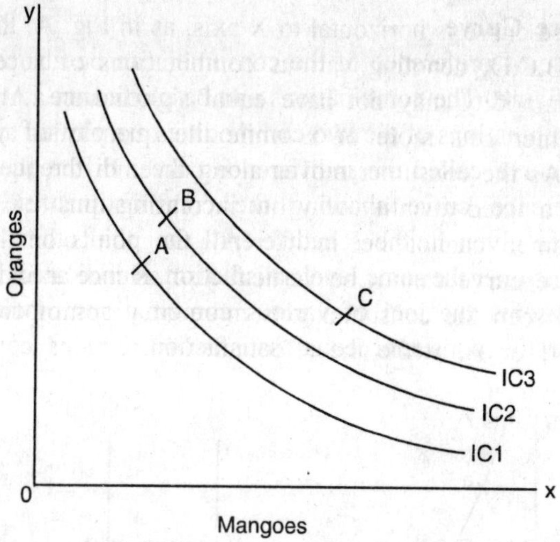

consumer the same satisfaction. At the point A on the IC1 the consumer demands 4 units of oranges and 2 units of mangoes. And on Point B on the curve IC_2 he demands 7 units of oranges and 4 units of mangoes and obtains a higher level of satisfaction. And Point C on the indifference curve IC_3 the consumer buys 6 units of oranges and 10 units of mangoes. The third combination gives more satisfaction than the combination 2 and 1. Thus it is seen that as the consumer prefers more units of both commodities, he moves on the higher indifference level and when he desires less units of both the commodities he moves down the indifference level. Thus the lower indifference curve gives him less satisfaction and higher indifference curve gives him a higher satisfaction. The set of indifference curves, which indicate the different levels of satisfaction, based on his scale of preference is called the indifference map.

CHARACTERISTICS OF THE INDIFFERENCE CURVES

1. Indifference curves slope down wards from left to right: The negative slope of the indifference curve indicates that when one commodity in the combination of another is increased, the amount of the other commodity is reduced. This is because the consumer has to remain on the same indifference curve. For instance if the indifference curve is horizontal to X axis, as in Fig. A. the various points A,B,C,D, denoting various combinations of x commodity and y commodity may not have equal significance. At point B, the consumer gets more of x while the quantity of y remains constant. As the consumer moves along the indifference curve he is getting a fixed quantity of y but increasing quantities of x. so the consumer cannot be indifferent. On the other hand the indifference curve cannot be vertical also as indicated in Fig. B. Here it is seen the consumer gets more of y commodity than at point C, B or A, while the x commodity remains constant. So

Fig 'A'

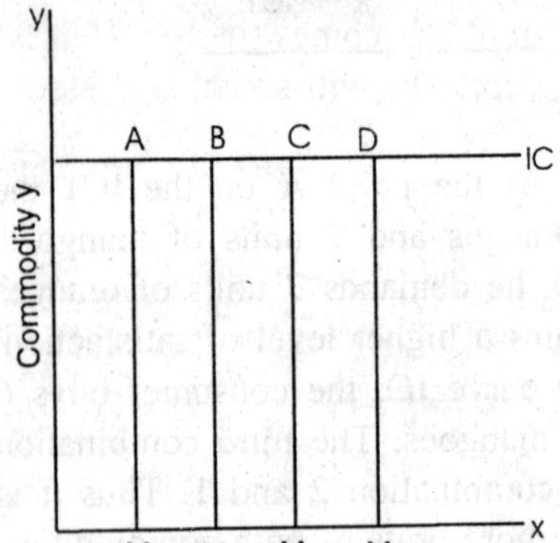

Fig 'B'

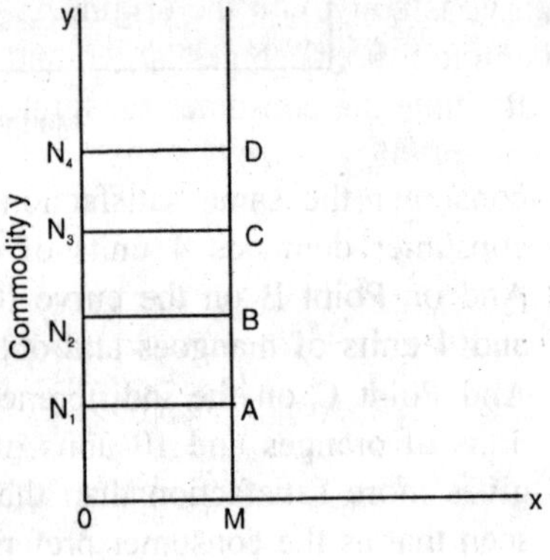

Fig 'C

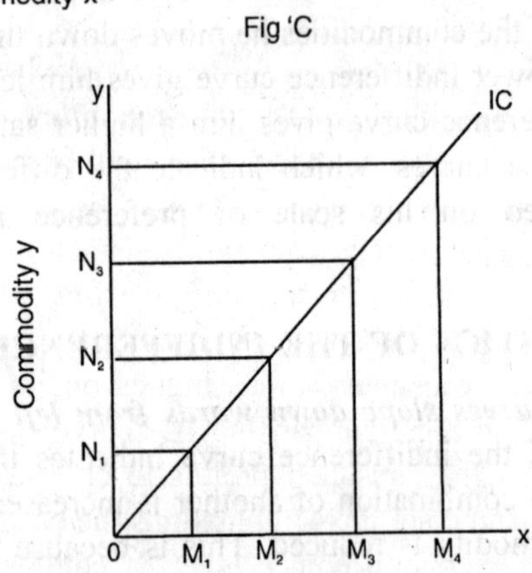

the consumer cannot be indifferent to various combinations as they refer different level of satisfaction. In the upward sloping curve too as shown in Fig. C, the different points on the curve differ in significance because as the consumer moves from A to B, he gets more of x and more of y commodities. And he cannot be indifferent to the combinations.

2. Indifference curves are convex to the origin: The slope of the indifference curve measures the marginal rate of substitution (MRS). Thus convexity illustrates the law of diminishing marginal rate of substitution. It states that the consumer values less of a commodity which has a large stock. In the figure the indifference curve is convex to the origin. As the consumer moves downwards, commodity x becomes larger, and that of y becomes smaller. Hence each time the consumer substitutes x for y he will sacrifice a lesser amount of y in exchange of x.

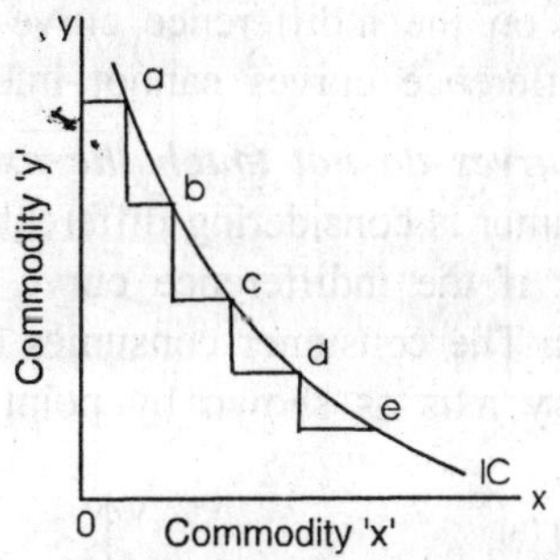

3. Indifference curves are parallel to each other: Indifference curves can never intersect each other. There will be no intersection between the two indifference curves. This is because each indifference curve represents a specific level of satisfaction. Indifference curves analysis is based on transitivity. Transitivity implies consistency in choice making. It is assumed a rational consumer would always prefer a larger quantity to a smaller one.

For instance 'b' in the figure in the IC_1 curve points a and b are combination that the consumer prefers to choose. And on the IC_2 curve, points a and c are the combinations the consumer prefers and he is on the higher indifference level. If combinations a and b give the same level satisfaction when he is on indifference curve

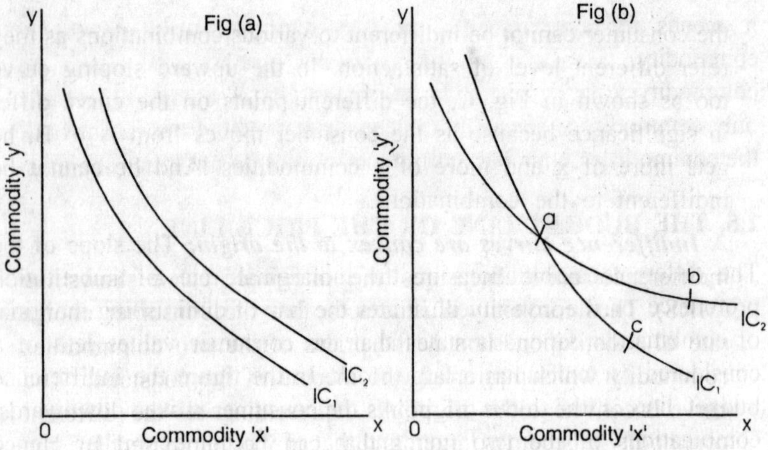

1, and if combinations a and b are equal, then a and c should be equal. But they cannot be equal, because a is the indifference curve 1 and c is on the indifference curve 2. it is can thus be inferred that indifference curves cannot intersect.

4. Indifference curves do not touch the axis: According to the analysis the consumer is considering different combinations of two commodities. But if the indifference curve touches either the y axis or the x axis. The consumer consumes only one commodity. If it touches the y axis as shown by point p in the figure (a),

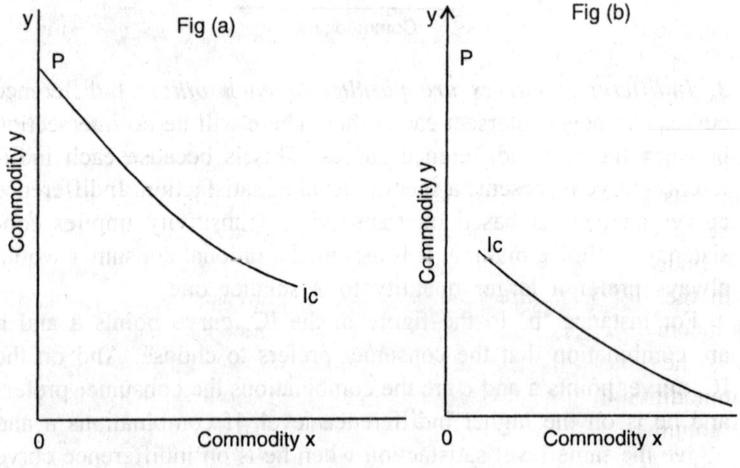

it means the consumer is satisfied with OP units of the y commodity. Similarly if the consumer prefers OM units of commodity x as indicated in the figure (b), it means he prefers only commodity x. In reality the consumer prefers to purchase both the commodities, thus the indifference curves do not touch the axis.

2.5. THE BUDGET LINE OR THE PRICE LINE

The different combinations on the indifference curve shows the preference of the consumer. It is seen that the consumer choice of combination depends on 1. the prices of the two commodities considered for consumption. 2. the income of the consumer. The budget line is the locus of points representing all the different combinations of the two goods that can be purchased by the consumer, given his money income and the prices of the two goods. For example let us assume our consumer has Rs 100 to be spent on two goods. If the price of M is 5 and the price of N is Rs 10, his alternative spending would be as illustrated in the table.

Combination	*Units of the commodity (M)*	*Units of commodity (N)*
A	20	0
B	14	3
C	10	5
D	0	10

When the consumer spends his income on commodity M, he gets 20 units of M and none of commodity of N, alternatively if he spends the entire income on commodity on N he obtains 10 units of N and none of commodity M. He can also change his combination and buy the two goods simultaneously by buying a little less of commodity N and a little more of commodity M or more of commodity of M and less of commodity N.
The budget line may also illustrated through a figure.

In the figure, point A denotes that if a consumer spends all his income on Y he can buy OA of Yand if he spends his income on x he can buy OB of X. Similarly if he buys both the commodities he spreads his income in such a way he buys both the commodities. Thus combination B shows that he prefers both

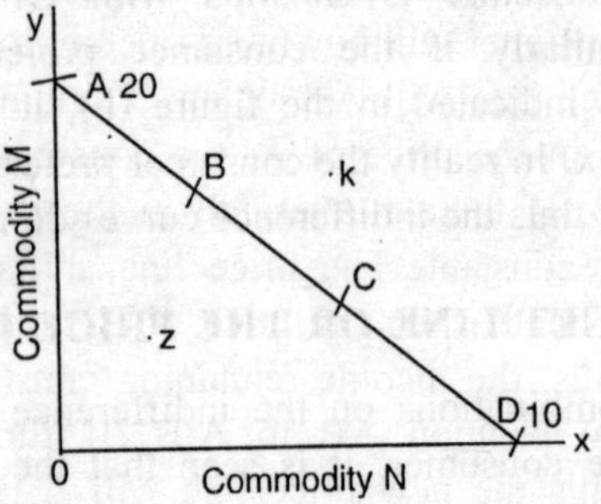

the commodities equally. Combination D shows that he prefers more of Y and less of X. Combination C shows that he prefers more of commodity X and less of commodity Y. Thus by joining points A and B we obtain the Budget line. The consumer cannot have any other combinations beyond this region for instance, point z shows that the consumer is under utilizing his income. Point K shows he prefers the combinations which is above his budget.

Changes in the Budget Line

There will be a change in the price line, when the price of either the two commodities changes or the income of the consumer changes.

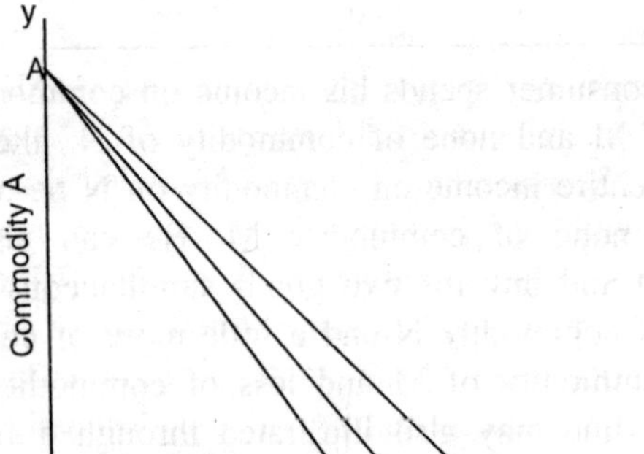

In the figure, the income of the consumer remains constant. The price of commodity A remains constant and that of commodity

B remains falls. The initial price line is AB. And when the price of B falls, the consumer will buy more of commodity B than before and the new price line will AB_1 or any combination on AB_1. As there no change in the price of A, the consumer purchases more of commodity B. If there further fall in the price of commodity B, A remaining constant. The price line shifts further to AB_2.

On the other hand when the price of B remains constant, and commodity A falls, the income remaining constant the price shift from its original position AB to A_1B. If further the price of commodity A falls the new price line will A_2B as shown in the figure below.

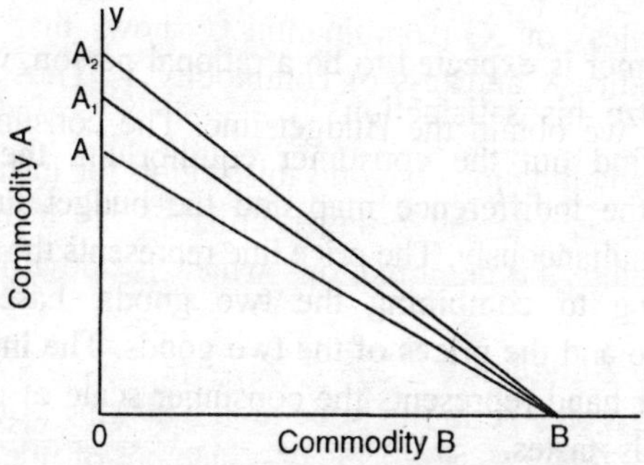

The price line shows a different shape when the income changes. As seen in the figure above, here it is assumed that income of the consumer changes and the prices of the two commodities remain unchanged. The original price line is AB. If the income of the consumer increases the prices of the two goods remaining unchanged, the price line will shift to higher position A_1B_1. This is because with increased income the consumer is able to purchase proportionally larger quantities of A and B. If the income of the consumer decreases without any change in the prices of the two goods, the price line will shift to the position A_2B_2. This is because at lower income tne consumer will proportionally purchase lesser quantities.

2.6. CONSUMER'S EQUILIBRIUM

The consumer attains equilibrium position when he obtains maximum satisfaction. When he reaches that point he would not be willing to reallocate his purchases as it would reduce his satisfaction.

Under the indifference curve approach the equilibrium position of the consumer is traced under the certain assumptions. They are:

- The consumer has a fixed amount of money to spend.
- He intends to buy a combination of two goods.
- All goods are homogenous and divisible.
- The consumer's scale of preference remains fixed throughout the analysis.
- The consumer has definite tastes and preferences. So he has a given scale of preference expressed through an indifference map.
- The consumer is expected to be a rational person, who seeks to maximize his satisfaction.

In order to find out the consumer equilibrium, the scale of preference i.e., the indifference map and the budget line should be considered simultaneously. The price line represents the budgetary constraint relating to combining the two goods, based on the consumer income and the prices of the two goods. The indifference map on the other hand represents the consumer scale of preference depending on his tastes.

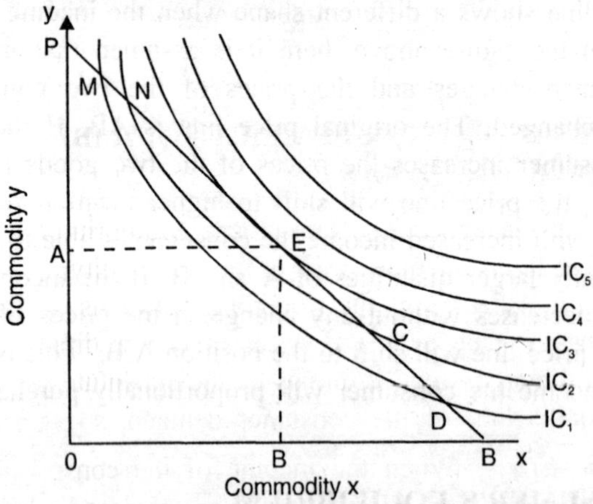

In the figure, commodity Y is measured on the Y axis, and commodity X is measured on the x axis. The price line PB shows the various combinations which are possible to be obtained by the consumer with his income and the prices of the two goods. By the bringing the price and the indifference map, we discover the combination of the two commodities, which is suitable for the consumer. The point of tangency represents the equilibrium position of the consumer. The maximum position he can reach is on the IC_3. The price line is tangential to IC_3 and tangency point E is the equilibrium position of the consumer. Any other combination of the two goods would lie on the a lower indifference curve and would obtain less satisfaction for the consumer. For the price line passes through the points MNCD. Point M lies on IC_1, N on IC_2, C on IC_2 and D on IC_1, all these points yield less satisfaction to the consumer. So point E is the maximum point of satisfaction the consumer could reach within the price-line PB. Points IC_4 and IC_5 are unattainable with the given resources. So the consumer will prefer remaining at point E getting OA units of commodity y and OB units of commodity x. This is the equilibrium position where the consumer gets maximum satisfaction.

At the equilibrium point, E is on the IC_3 and the price line PB are tangent to each other. Hence at the equilibrium point the marginal rate of substitution between two goods is equal to the ratio of their price.

that is: $$MRS_{xy} = \frac{P_x}{P_y}$$

CHANGES IN THE CONSUMER'S EQUILIBRIUM AND ITS EFFECT ON DEMAND

In analysing the concept of consumer's equilibrium, we assumed that the consumer's income, price of the commodity, and substitutes to remain constant. In the foregoing analysis we would be considering the change in the prices of commodities, the income of the consumer, change in prices of the substitutes and its effect on the equilibrium of the consumer demand.

1. Income Effect: When the income of the consumer increases he is in a better off position to buy more commodities and obtain greater satisfaction. Alternatively if his income decreases he reduces his purchases to lesser quantities. Thus the income effect may be defined as the effect of changes in the money income on a consumer's equilibrium position in the purchases of a single good or a combination of goods, assuming that prices of goods and taste remaining constant. The income effect also refers to the change in the demand for a commodity resulting from a change in the income of the consumer and prices of goods being constant.

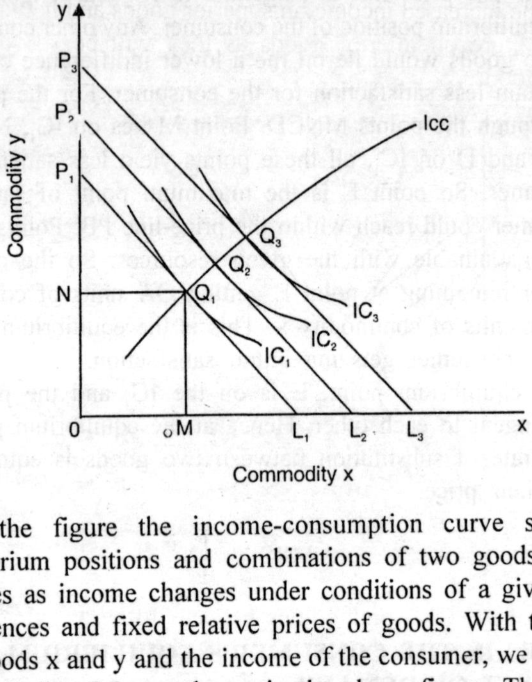

In the figure the income-consumption curve shows how equilibrium positions and combinations of two goods (x and y) changes as income changes under conditions of a given scale of preferences and fixed relative prices of goods. With the price of two goods x and y and the income of the consumer, we have drawn the price line P_1L_1 as shown in the above figure. The consumer is in a equilibrium position point Q_1 on the indifference curve IC_1. when the income of the consumer increases he will be in a position to buy OP_2 of commodity y and OL_1 of commodity x. And his new budget line will be P_2L_2, and the new equilibrium position will be Q_2. Suppose his income further increases, his price line shift to a still higher position indicated by P_3L_3. The consumer is in a equilibirium point Q_3 on the indifference curve IC_3.

When the various equilibrium points are connected together, we obtain what is called the Income Consumption Curve. Thus the income consumption curve is the locus of equilibrium points at various levels of consumer's income. It traces the income effect on the quantities purchased.

The income effect may be positive or negative. Income effect is said to be positive when the purchase or consumption of a commodity increase with increase in income. Income effect can be negative when the consumer purchases less of goods with the increases in his income. Such goods are inferior goods. When the income of the consumer increases, the tendency on his part would to spend the increased income on superior goods and he will reduce his expenditure on inferior goods as they will be substituted by superior goods.

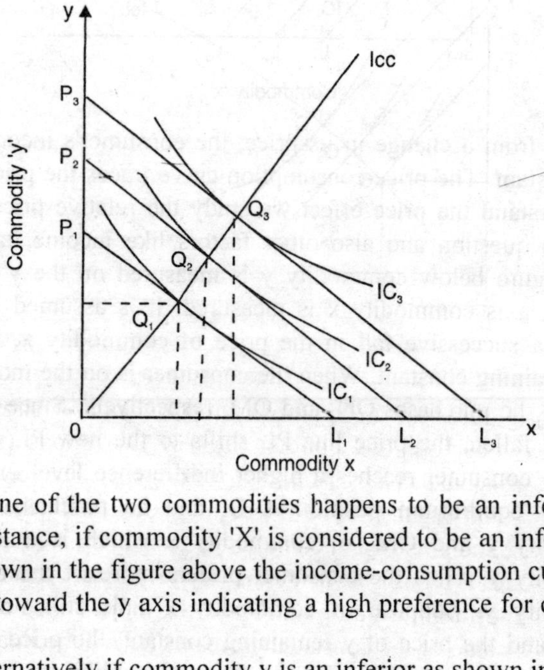

If one of the two commodities happens to be an inferior good. For instance, if commodity 'X' is considered to be an inferior good. As shown in the figure above the income-consumption curve would move toward the y axis indicating a high preference for commodity y.

Alternatively if commodity y is an inferior as shown in the figure below the consumer may not demand that commodity, instead he would demand more of commodity x. Hence income consumption curve would move towards the x axis indicating the consumers higher preference for commodity x, as shown in the figure below.

*2. **Price Effect:*** The consumer reaction to a change in the price of a commodity , other things like income, tastes of the consumer remaining constant is called price effect. The price effect can also be referred to the change in quantity demanded of a commodity

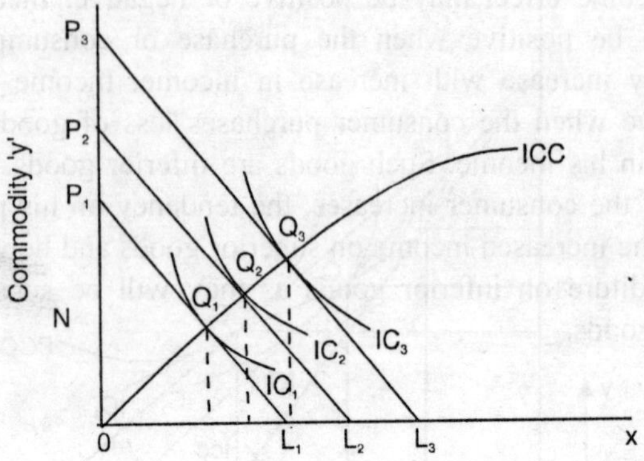

resulting from a change in its price, the consumer's income being held constant. The price-consumption curve traces the price effect. To understand the price effect we study the relative prices of the goods in question and also other factors like income, tastes etc. In the figure below commodity y is measured on the y axis and on the x axis commodity x is measured. It is assumed here that there is a successive fall in the price of commodity x, the price of y remaining constant. When the consumer is on the indifference curve IC_1 he purchases ON_1 and OM_1 respectively. Since the price of x has fallen, the price line PL shifts to the new PL_1 position. Here the consumer reaches a higher indifference level that is IC_2. His new equilibrium position is Q_2 and he purchases ON_2 of commodity y and OM_2 of commodity x which is a little than commodity y. Thus the consumer prefers more of x and less of commodity y. Suppose of commodity x falls still further, the income and the price of y remaining constant, the price line shift to the new position PL_2. The consumers equilibrium remains at Q_3, where he more of commodity x than commodity y.

When the equilibrium points Q_1, Q_2, and Q_3 are joined together we obtain what is called the price-consumption curve. The course of this curve shows the price effect on the consumption of the commodities.

3. ***Substitution Effect*** When the consumer is demanding a substitutable commodity, he would compare the price of the two in consideration and demand a commodity whose price is less. Such

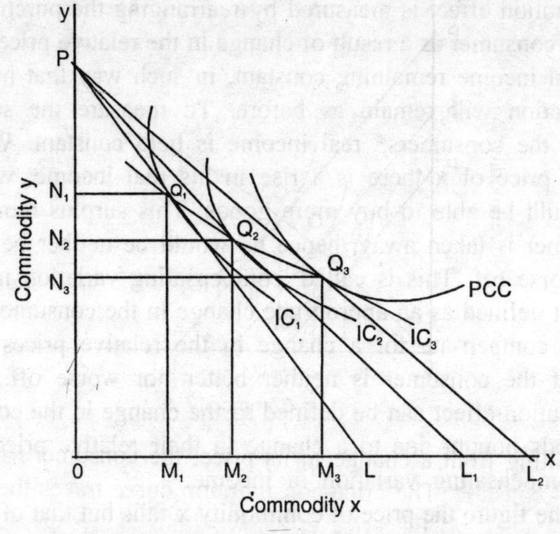

effect of demand of the consumer is known as substitution effect. The substitution effect is the change in the quantity demanded of a commodity resulting from a change in its price relative to the prices of other commodities, the consumer's real income or satisfaction level being held constant.

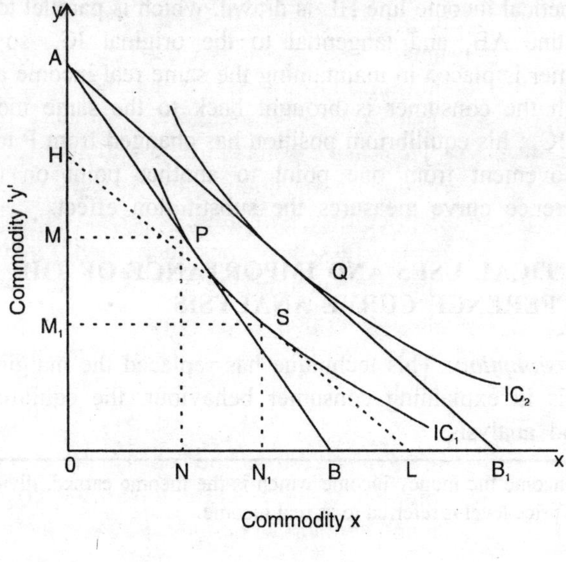

Substitution effect is measured by rearranging the purchases made by the consumer as a result of change in the relative price of goods, his real income remaining constant, in such way that his level of satisfaction will remain as before. To measure the substitution effect, the consumers* real income is held constant. With a fall in the price of x there is a rise in his real income, with which he would be able to buy more goods. This surplus money of the consumer is taken away, hence he would be neither be better off nor worse off. This is called 'compensating variation in income'. Thus it defined as an appropriate change in the consumer's income would compensate for a change in the relative prices of goods so that the consumer is neither better nor worse off. Thus the substitution effect can be defined as the change in the combination of goods bought due to a change in their relative prices, despite the compensating variation in income.

In the figure the price of commodity x falls but that of y remains constant. The point S denotes that the consumer buys ON_1 of X and OM_1 of Y. He has substituted NN_1 of X for MM_1 of Y. The initial equilibrium of the consumer is at point X. Where the price line AB is tangent to IC_1. He buys OM of Y and ON of X. When the price of x falls while that of Y remains unchanged, the price line will shift to AB_1. To measure the pure substitution effect, a hypothetical income line HL is drawn, which is parallel to the new price line AB_1 and tangential to the original IC_2, so that the consumer is placed in maintaining the same real income as before. Though the consumer is brought back to the same indifference curve IC_{21}, his equilibrium position has changed from P to S. Thus the movement from one point to another point on the same indifference curve measures the substitution effect.

PRACTICAL USES AND IMPORTANCE OF THE INDIFFERENCE CURVE ANALYSIS

1. Consumption: This technique has replaced the marginal utility analysis in explaining consumer behaviour, the equilibrium and demand analysis.

---

* real income the money income which is the income earned, divided by the general price level is referred to as real income.

2. Scientific: The indifference curve analysis is based on the principle of marginal rate of substitution. This concept is more superior to the law of marginal utility, because it considers two goods together and expresses it as ratio of physical units.

3. Production: The indifference technique is made use of in finding out the producers equilibrium. Just as the indifference curve is for the consumer, the equal product curve is for the producer.

4. Exchange: In the field of exchange, indifference curves can be used to determine the position of equilibrium when two individuals are entering into a market. The technique has shown the manner in which exchange can take place between two parties where their preferences of the goods are given.

5. Taxation: The principle of indifference curve technique is applied in the field of taxation in public finance. Which is used to judge the welfare effects of a direct and indirect tax on the individual.

6. Savings: This technique can also be utilized in the field of savings. The indifference curves shows that the preference of an individual between present and future goods. His decision to save depends on desire on present goods over future goods. It is also used in the field of index numbers to show the standard of living of the consumer in two different periods with different levels.

2.7. CONSUMER'S SURPLUS

The concept of consumer's surplus has been introduced to indicate consumer's gain from the goods he purchases from the market. At times the consumer may derive a greater satisfaction from the commodity, than the price paid for the commodity.

This is termed as the consumer's surplus. Dupuit first introduced the concept, later it was reformulated by Marshall. According to him, "the excess of price which a person would be willing to pay rather than go without the thing, over that which he actually does pay is the economic measure of this surplus of satisfaction. It may be called Consumer's surplus". A consumer may be willing to pay the price for a commodity till the point where marginal utility derived is higher than the price paid for the commodity. Consumer's surplus is therefore measured as the difference between the maximum price the consumer is willing to pay for the commodity and the actual market price charged for it. Consumer's surplus may also be defined as "the difference between the total amount of money the consumer would have been willing to pay for a quantity of a commodity and the amount he actually had to pay for it".

The doctrine of consumer surplus is based on the law of diminishing marginal utility, where the utility of the consumer gradually decreases as he keeps on increasing the demand for a commodity.

The consumer surplus an be measured through a formula.

Consumer's Surplus = Total Utility – (Price × Quantity)

In symbolic terms: **Consumer's Surplus (CS) = TU – (P × Q)**

Where TU = total utility
Q = quantity if the commodity
P = Price.

Alternatively consumer's surplus = Price prepared to pay – Actual price paid.

Unit of commodity Z	*Marginal utility MU*	*market price Rs*	*Consumer surplus = Prep to pay – Actual mkt. price*
1	50	20	30
2	40	20	20
3	32	20	12
4	20	20	0
total 4 units	142	80	62

thus CS = TU – (P × Q)
= 142 – (20 × 4)
= 62

The concept of consumer's surplus is explained in the above schedule. The price of commodity z is assumed to be Rs 20 per unit. By buying the first unit the consumer obtains 50 units of marginal utility. The surplus which he willing to pay is Rs 30. When he consumes the second unit. The price remaining the same, the consumer's marginal utility is 40. The consumer surplus here is Rs 30. It is thus seen here that the consumer surplus for the commodity gradually goes down and when he buys the 4 units the marginal utility is equal to the price paid, the consumer surplus is 0. Hence the consumer would not progress to buy commodities beyond this point. It can also be noticed that the concept of consumer surplus behaves in a similar fashion as the law of diminishing utility.

Diagrammatic illustration

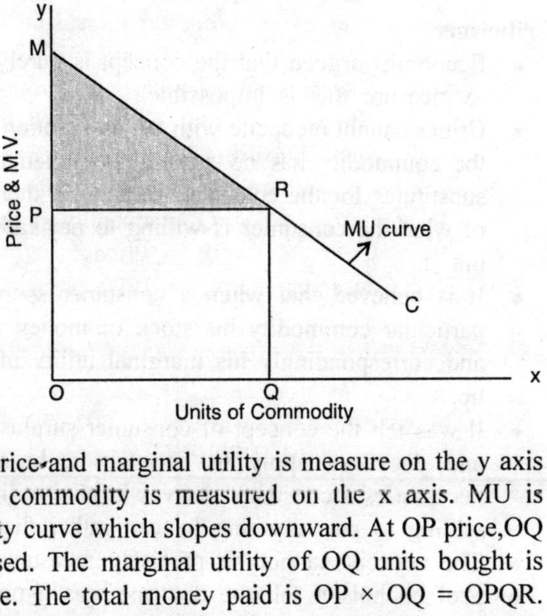

In the figure price and marginal utility is measure on the y axis and units of the commodity is measured on the x axis. MU is the marginal utility curve which slopes downward. At OP price,OQ units are purchased. The marginal utility of OQ units bought is equal to OP price. The total money paid is OP × OQ = OPQR. The total utility derived = OMRQ. Thus consumer's surplus = OMRQ – OPRQ = MRP.

Assumptions

There are certain basic assumptions which underlie the concept of consumer surplus.

- The consumer's surplus is based on the cardinal utility which measures utility in terms of units.
- The concept of consumer's surplus involves ceteris paribus assumption underlying the law of diminishing marginal utility.
- Since the concept is derived on the basis of demand for the commodity, all assumptions made for the demand analysis

are equally applicable here. In drawing the demand curve we assume that the tastes, preferences, of the consumer remain constant and the study is made only with reference to change in price of a particular commodity.

- The utility of a commodity depends on the quantity of commodity alone. Each commodity is treated alone.

Criticisms

- Economist argued that the concept is purely subjective, and to measure this is impossible.
- Critics cannot reconcile with the assumption of Marshall that the commodity has no substitutes. When there are lots of substitutes for the consumer to choose, there is no question of what the consumer is willing to pay rather than go with out it.
- It is believed that when a consumer spends money on a particular commodity his stock of money will get reduced and correspondingly his marginal utility of money will go up.
- It was felt the concept of consumer surplus is meaning less and does not apply to necessaries, because in case of necessaries a consumer derives infinite utility and would be willing to pay anything he can rather than go without it.
- The concept cannot be precisely measured.
- Prof Nicholson felt the doctrine was hypothetical. In case of articles like diamonds possessing scarcity and value, consumer's surplus seemed to be unsubstantial. Thus it was felt the concept was invalid in case of luxuries goods.

Importance of the Concept

- The concept of consumer's surplus is useful in clarifying the paradox of value by distinguishing the value-in-use and value-in-exchange. Consumer surplus depends on the difference between total utility and price and price depends on marginal utility. A high consumer surplus thus implies value-in-use as compared to the value-in exchange of a commodity. In articles salt, water the value-in use more compared to value-in exchange, but in case diamonds value-in exchange is greater that its use.

- It is useful in determining the price of a commodity, by analysing the preference of the consumer, his likes and dislikes, the price of the commodity can be altered.
- This concept is widely accepted in welfare economics. As it helps to compare the effects of a given change in the price of any commodity on different classes of people.
- The concept of consumer surplus is useful in international trade.
- It is of greater significance to the exchequer in determining indirect taxation. Taxes on commodities can be changed depending on their consumer surplus.

2.8. CONSUMER SOVEREIGNTY

The freedom of the consumer to select the goods of his own choice is termed as consumer sovereignty. It refers to the free act of consumption. The concept of consumer sovereignty indirectly states the all acts of production ultimately depends on the consumer, it is he who decides the type and form of production because of his purchasing power.

In the capitalist economy, it attaches great importance, as it gives accords special value to individual liberty in purchasing commodities to satisfy their wants. In a free market economy, a person can buy whatever commodity he likes by spending his income. Consumer sovereignty under capitalism also acts as a main determinant in the production process. This is because production is entirely guided by the demand and consumption of the commodity. The role of the consumers preference is thus emphasized, with regard to the decision making of producers for the allocation and use of the means of production. Thus the consumer is treated as a 'sovereign' or a king in a capitalist economy.

Thus under capitalism the producer's main aim would be to maximize profits. Thus he would also benefit by producing those goods which would enable him to earn supernormal profits. Profits however are also determined by prices. They are inturn determined by the market forces of demand and supply. Hence the producers will use their resources to produce such goods, which would obtain for them goods markets and profits. When the consumer's demand for a commodity rises, the initial market supply being inelastic, the market prices rises, implying a rise in profits. Production being profit oriented leads to expansion of output. Similarly, when the demand for a commodity falls, the total demand for these goods contracts, hence prices and profits decline. Producers will cut down the output of such goods and the community at large derives adjustment between demand for productive factors such as land, labour and capital from the demand for consumer goods. Hence the allocation of economic resources of different sectors and industries is determined by the consumers demand expressed in terms of money they spend. Thus in a market the producers have to consider the preferences, tastes of the consumers while deciding the type of commodity to be produced. Since there are a very large number of consumers with their individual choices, when production takes place accordingly, the diversification becomes enormous. This encourages competition and innovations to satisfy the diverse needs and choices or the tastes of many people.

Socialists however state that the concept of consumer sovereignty has little meaning in a capitalist economy. This is because there exist wider disparities of income and wealth. They opine that if money is only factor determining production, then it would be only the rich consumers who could afford to procure the goods. Some economists are of the view that wants are artificially fabricated by advertising and other marketing techniques.

Limitations

- *Ignorance*: Most of the consumers are ignorant about the type of goods and their availability and due to their ignorance they may not be able to express their choice.
- *Influence*: Consumers are carried away by other influences like the advertisement, marketing strategies of suppliers, and they hence do not freely express their opinion.
- *Income*: There exists different classes of customers in the economy, if the income is limited, he would not be in a position to express his choice, rather he would buy what ever commodity is available at affordable price.
- *Regulations*: Government laws and regulations restricts consumer sovereignty. Rationing of commodities, heavy taxation effect the consumer preference of a commodity.

- *Markets*: Competitive situations also affect consumer choice. For instance in a monopoly situation, he has to either buy the commodity or live without it, because the commodity has no substitutes in the form of commodity or competitors, but on the other hand in a monopolistic situation he is free to choose the commodity according to his taste.

Despite many limitations, which effect its standing, consumer sovereignty, still plays a important role in effecting the production and distribution of a commodity.

MODEL QUESTIONS

Short questions

1. What is meant by consumer surplus?
2. Explain the difference between average and marginal utility.
3. Explain the term utility.
4. Define the law of diminishing marginal utility.
5. Explain the term consumer sovereignty.
6. What is a budget line?
7. What is meant by consumption?

Essay Questions

1. Explain the different properties of an indifference curve.
2. Explain the law of equimarginal ulility and its practical utility.
3. What are the limitations of consumer sovereignty?
4. Analyse the demerits of the law of diminishing marginal utility.

3

Demand Analysis

3.1. MEANING

The theory of demand is related to the economic activities of a consumer. The process through which a consumer obtains the goods and services, he wants to consume is known as Demand. Demand is the desire or want for something. But in economics, it is given a special meaning. Demand is the desire or want backed up by money. It is considered the effective desire which is backed up by the ability and willingness to pay for it. According to Hibdon "Demand means the various quantities of goods that would be purchased per time period at different prices in a given market". Thus three things are necessary for demand to exist:

1. Price of the commodity.
2. The unit of the commodity the consumers are prepared to buy per unit of time.
3. A Given time.

According to Benham "The demand for anything at a given price is the amount of it which will be bought per unit of time at that price". Thus want for a commodity without possessing money to buy it or unwillingness to pay a given price will not constitute a demand for that commodity. For instance a pauper's wish for a car. Likewise a miser's desire for the lavish food. However rich he may be he will not be willing to demand such a food.

Thus demand can be algebraically written as:

Demand = Desire + Ability to pay + willingness to pay for commodity.

It can also be stated as $D = f(p)$, where the demand for a product functionally depends on its price of the commodity.

Demand is always related to price and time: Demand is not an absolute term. Demand for a commodity should always have a reference to price and time. Thus economists always mention the amount for a commodity with reference to a particular price and specific time period, such a month, a year etc.

3.2. FEATURES OF DEMAND

1. *Difference between desire and demand*: Demand is the amount of a commodity for which a consumer has the willingness and the ability to buy.
2. *Relationship between demand and price*: Demand is always at a price. Unless price is stated, the amount demanded has no meaning. The consumer must know both the price and the commodity.
3. *Demand at a point of time*: The amount demanded must refer to some period of time. Such as 10 quintals of wheat per month. The amount demanded and price must refer to a particular date.

Thus demand for a commodity refers to the amount of it, which will be bought per unit of time at a particular price.

3.3. DEMAND SCHEDULE

Demand schedule is a tabular statement, which shows how much of a commodity is demanded at a particular market at different prices. According to Benham "a full account of the demand for any goods in a given market at a given time should state what the volume of sales would be at each of a series of prices". Such an account, taking the form of a tabular statement is known as demand schedule. A demand schedule may be an individual demand schedule and market demand schedule. The former refers to quantities demanded by a consumer at different prices. While the market demand schedule speaks about the aggregate demand for commodities in the market at different price levels.

The individual and market demand schedules are explained with suitable examples.

1. Individual Demand Schedule

India : ideal demand schedule refers to a single consumers demand of a commodity at varying prices

Individual demand schedule for eggs

Price of eggs per dozen	*Quantity of eggs demanded (per month)*
15	4
13	5
11	7
10	9
9	12

The above schedule explains an individuals demand for eggs for a month. When the price is Rs. 15 he demands 4 dozens. When the price falls to Rs. 13 he demands 5 dozens. Still when the prices of eggs fall. He demands 7 dozens of eggs and when the price falls to Rs. 10 he demands 9 dozens and when the price is Rs. 9 he demands 12 dozens. The above schedule clearly states that the consumer demands less of the commodity when the price is high but gradually increasing his purchasing power for the same when the price of the commodity falls.

2. Market Demand Schedule

The market demand schedule is the demand schedule of the aggregate demand for all individuals in the market.

Market Demand Schedule for Butter

Price of Butter	*Demand of consumer A*	*Demand of consumer B*	*Demand of consumer C*	*Market Demand*
90	2	4	5	11
75	3	6	8	17
55	5	9	12	26

The individual and market demand schedule can also be explained through figures.

The demand schedule when represented diagrammatically is known as individual demand curve. The figure below depicts the individual demand curve. The individual demand curve shows the

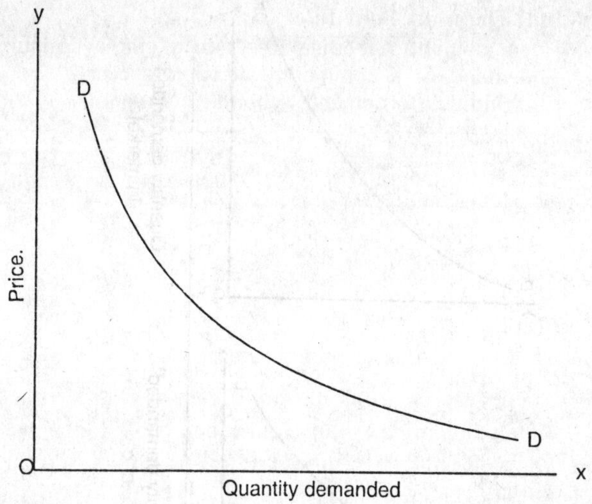

maximum price which an individual consumer or a household would be prepared to pay for different amounts of the good.

The market demand schedule

Figure explains the market demand curve. The quantity demanded in the market is the sum of individual demand of all consumers at that price. The market demand curve for a given commodity is the horizontal summation of the demand of individual consumers as shown in the figure on p. 70. In the figure below. It is also noticed that the market demand curve is a slightly flatter bigger curve than the other three demand curves, but the movement of the market demand curve takes the same position as of the other demand curves. Thus indicating the summation of the individual demand curves in the market.

3.4. DEMAND FUNCTION

The demand for a commodity depends on the desire and the capability of a individual to buy the commodity. Thus the functional relationship between the demand for a commodity and its various determinants can be expressed though a demand function which may be expressed as:

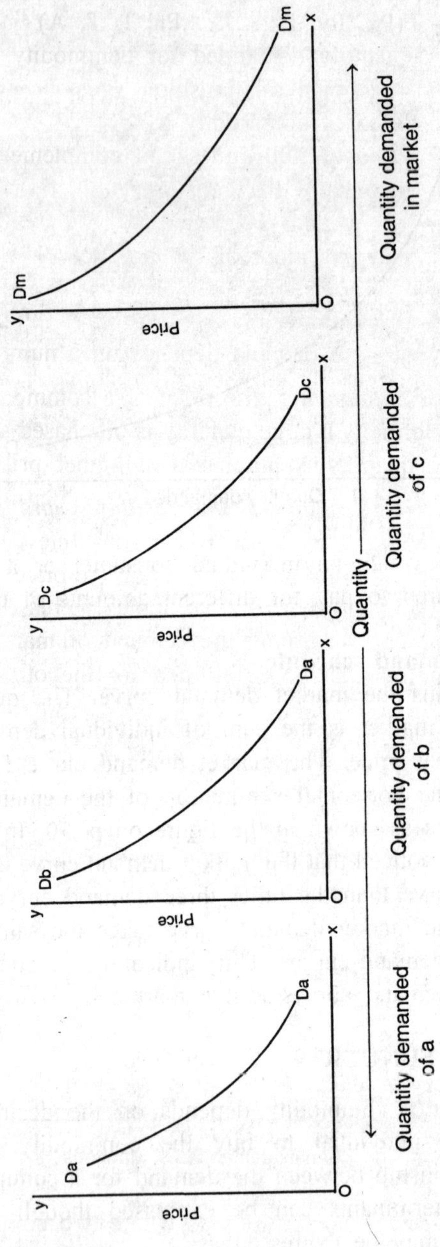
y
Da
Price
O
x
Da
Quantity demanded of a
y
Db
Price
O
x
Da
Quantity demanded of b
y
Dc
Price
O
x
Dc
Quantity demanded of c
Quantity
y
Dm
Price
O
x
Dm
Quantity demanded in market

Dx = F(Px, Py, Pz.........Pn, I, T, A)

Where Dx = Quantity demanded for commodity x.

F = Functional relationship.

Px = Price of commodity x.

Py = Price of Substitutes and complementary goods.

I = Income of the consumer.

T = Tastes and preference.

A = Advertisement of the product.

Determinants of Demand

The determinants of demand depends on a number of factors:

1. Price of the commodity: The price of a commodity influences the demand. Normally a large quantity is purchased at lower prices and a smaller quantity is purchased at higher prices.

2. Price of related commodities-substitutes and complements: When the commodity in usage has a substitute commodity, the demand for a commodity here depends on the price of a substitute commodity. Eg: when the price of apples increases the price of mangoes remaining the same, the demand of mangoes increases as one commodity can be substituted for the other.

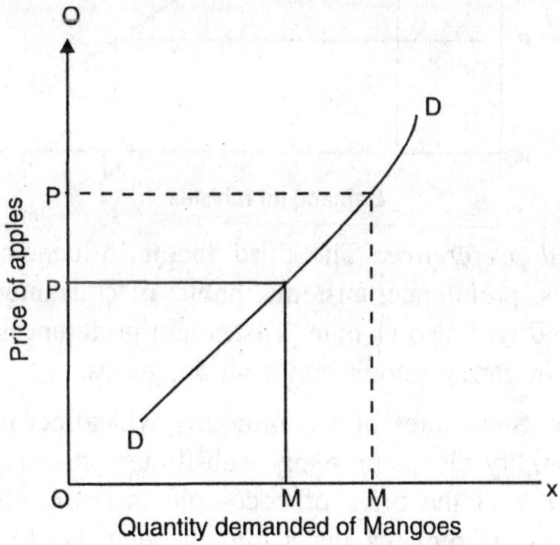

In case of complementary goods where two commodities have to be demanded together. It is seen here that as the price of one complementary goods increases the demand for its complementary decreases.

Factors influencing Demand

*1. **Large number of consumers:*** Larger the consumers, the larger will be the demand for that commodity. The size of the population also influences the demand for the commodity.

*2. **Income:*** Demand depends on the level of income and wealth of the consumers. A rise in income and wealth of consumers will push up demand, while a decline in the levels of income and wealth will decrease the demand for the commodity.

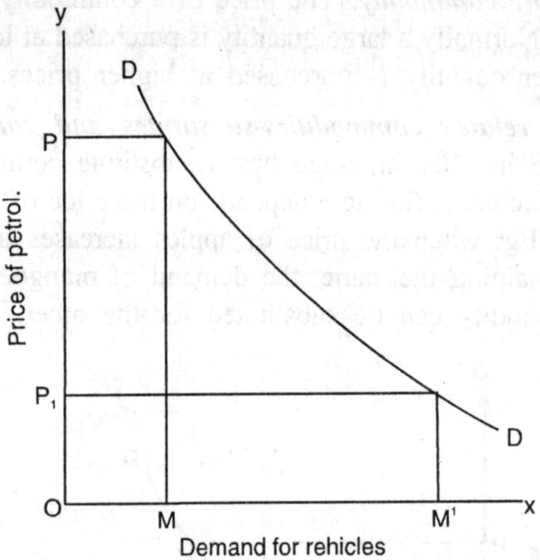

*3. **Tastes and preference:*** The third factor influencing demand refers to tastes, preference, customs, habits of consumers. If these change demand will also change. Tastes and preferences will have full demand in fancy goods and fashion goods.

*4. **Substitutes:*** Substitutes of a commodity will affect the demand of the commodity. It there many substitutes, the demand gets divided. For e.g. if the price of coco-cola increases the price of its substitute pepsi remains the same, the demand for the pepsi will increase.

*5. **Future expectations:*** If the consumers expect the prices of commodities to increase in the future, at the present prices they may demand more commodities. If the consumers anticipate shortage of goods due to unforeseen circumstances they might increase the demand at current prices.

6. Weather conditions: The demand for certain commodities may change due to weather conditions. For example the demand for woollen clothing will increase in winter and demand for cotton clothes will increase in summer.

3.5. LAW OF DEMAND

The law of demand indicates an inverse relationship between the price of a commodity and quantity demanded in the market. It may be stated as "other things remaining constant, with an increase in price the quantity demanded falls and with a fall in price the quantity demanded extends". The law in simple words states an indirect relationship between quantity demanded and price. According to Marshall, "the greater the amount to be sold the smaller must be the price at which it is offered in order that it may find purchasers or in other words, the amount demanded increases with a fall in price and diminishes with a rise in price".

The law of demand can be explained through a simple demand Schedule.

Price	*Quantity demanded*
20	15
10	23
7	35

In the above table it is seen when price of commodity increases quantity demanded decreases. For example when the price of the commodity if Rs. 10 quantity demanded is 23 units. When the price increases to Rs. 20 the quantity demanded is 15 units. On the other hand when the price falls to Rs 7 quantity demanded increases to 35 units. This schedule clearly shows that price and quantity are inversely proportional. This is also because at a given point the consumer may be desiring to buy many commodities and hence he cannot buy one commodity. Since he has to buy other commodities, he cannot purchase one commodity when it is highly priced.

Other things remaining constant, implies that the law of demand allows only price to play a major role keeping the other factors constant. The low of demand can also be explained through a figure.

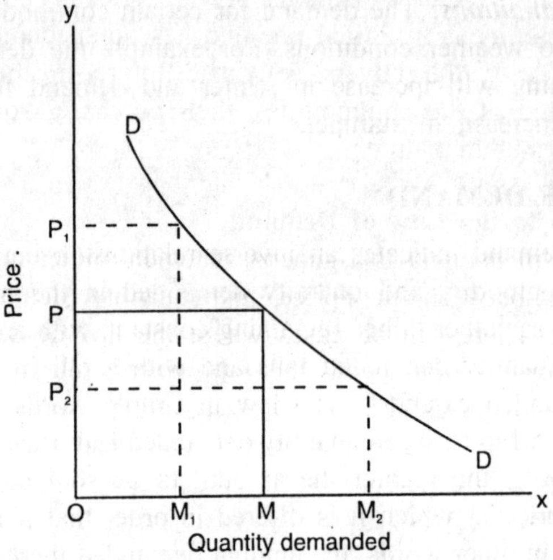

In the figure below, when the price is OP. Quantity demanded is OM. When the price increases to OP_1, the quantity demanded decreases to OM_1, on the other hand when the price falls to OP_2 the quantity demanded increases to OM_2.

Thus the figure explains the inverse relationship between price and quantity demanded keeping the other factors constant. Thus the demand curve slopes down wards from left to right indicating the increase relationship between price and quantity demanded.

Assumptions to the Law of demand

Assumptions refer to certain preconditions fixed to the economic laws and theories to make them more operational in nature.

- The law of demand assumes the income of the consumer to remain the same. The consumer's tastes, preference are expected to remain the same.
- it is also assumed that future demand for commodities remains the same.
- prices of other substitute goods are expected to be remain

unchanged. If there is a change in the prices of related goods it may reflect on the demand of commodity in question.

- the level of taxation and policy of the government is assumed to be constant.
- the law requires that the given price change for the commodity is a normal one and has no speculative consideration. If the buyers anticipate future in the prices or demand of the commodities, their purchase would become abnormal in nature.

Exceptions to the Law of Demand

The law of demand is a general statement indicating a indirect relationship between the price and quantity demanded of a commodity. There can be cases where the law of demand does not hold good. It can be in the following cases.

1. **Veblen effect:** Thorstein Veblen in his doctrine stated that there were certain category of people who demanded commodities not because of their intrinsic value but because of the status attached to the commodity. Veblen referred this effect as conspicuous consumption. It was also found that when the prices of such increased people demanded them more and when the prices increased people demanded them less.
2. **Speculative effect:** When consumers speculate a future shortage supply of goods they might intend to buy commodities even they are highly priced. On the other hand if they expect prices to increase in the future they might demand more at the current prices.
3. **Giffen Paradox:** Sir Robert Giffen in the 19 century found that British labourers bought more of the inferior commodity that were potatoes. When the income of the labourers increased they shifted to a superior commodity which was meat and hence they bought more of meat and less of the inferior commodity which was potato. The effect of people demanding inferior goods when their income was less and demanding a superior commodity when their income increased was called the giffen paradox.
4. **Habits:** When consumers get habituated to a certain habit

of consuming a particular commodity, they would intend to buy the same commodity even at a higher price.

Thus in exceptional cases as ones stated the law of demand does not hold good.

Why does the demand curve have a Negative slope?

The demand curve is convex curve, which slopes from left to right downwards. This indicates that more is demanded at a lower price. The question why the demand curve has to slope downwards is because of various reasons.

1. **Operation of the law of diminishing marginal utility:** When a consumer purchases more quantities of a commodity, his utility for a commodity diminishes. That is the marginal utility of additional units of commodity purchased by the consumers gives him lesser and lesser satisfaction. The consumer will not be willing to pay for the commodity which gives him lesser satisfaction. Therefore the consumer will not buy a large quantity unless the price is low. For example the consumer buys fruits. Lets us assume the price of a kg of apples is Rs 40 and he buys a kg of apples and obtains 40 units of satisfaction. He will not the next of apples, because that would give him less marginal utility.

   On the other hand when the price of apples fall he would be willing to buy more of apples as he would get more satisfaction, by spending a little less than before. Thus when price increases, the consumer must reduce his purchase by reducing those units of the commodity which yield to him less utility than the price. Thus the price paid by the consumers is measures the marginal utility of the commodity.

2. **Income Effect:** As the price of the commodity falls, the real income of the consumer increases. He now has more money in his hand to spend on the commodities. A part of the money gained can be utilized on buying more commodities. The consumer here need not buy the same commodity, instead he can opt for another commodity. Similarly if the price increases, the consumers income in effect is reduced and he has to curtail his expenditure on the commodity. So, the quantity purchased falls. This is called income effect. For instance let us Mr K assume stays in a five star hotel whenever he is on a business

trip, which can last for a period of three days to one week. If suddenly there is a slight fall in his profit. He would prefer to stay in a three star hotel, since the rate is less compared to a five star hotel.

3. **Substitution Effect** When the consumer consume two substitutable commodities, when the price of one of the commodities rises it can be substituted for another. For example when the price of wheat increases it can be substituted for rice. It is found that substitution effect has more stronger effect than the income effect, as the consumer would be willing to demand different commodities than the same commodity.
4. **Utility:** There are certain commodities, which can be put to different uses. For example, Electricity can be used for different purposes. If the price of power per unit increases its uses can be decreased. On the other hand if the price decreases it utility can be increased.

3.6. ANALYSIS OF DEMAND

It is seen that price plays an important role in determining the demand of a commodity. Though there are factors that play a role in determining the demand, it is seen the price factor influences the demand for a commodity drastically. The analysis of demand thus tries to find how demand changes due to effect of price and also due to effect of other factors.

This can be analysed in two ways:

1. Extension and contraction of Demand.
2. Increase and Decrease of Demand.

1. Extension and Contraction of Demand

The movement of demand along the same demand curve is referred to as extension and contraction of demand. When the price increases the demand for a commodity decreases, this is referred to 'contraction of demand'. On the other hand when the price decreases demand for the commodity increases this is known as the 'extension of demand'.

The extension and contraction of demand can be explained through the above figure.

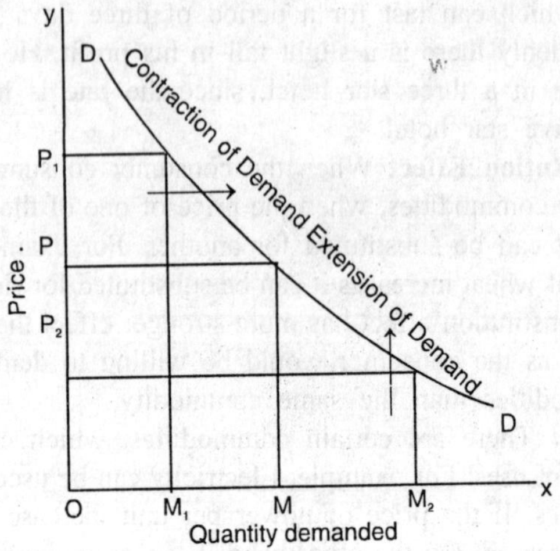

In the above figure the price of the commodity is measured on the Y axis and quantity demanded is measured on X axis. DD is demand curve that slopes downwards. The initial price charged is OP and quantity demanded is OM. When the price increases to OP_1, the quantity demanded a decrease to OM_1, this movement of the demand curve from OM to OM_1 is known as contraction of demand. Similarly when the price decreases, to OP_2 the quantity demanded increases to OM_2. This movement of the demand curve from OM to OM_2 is called extension of demand. The extension and contraction of demand indicates that both price and demand changes and that they inversely related to each other. Another factor to be noted in this analysis is price plays a dominant role in determining the demand for a commodity and other factors do not play a dominant role.

2. Increase and Decrease of Demand

The change (Increase and decrease) of demand due to the influence of other factors apart from price is known increase and decrease of demand. 'Increase of demand' implies that at any given price a larger amount is demanded or less amount of quantity is demanded.

In the figure X axis measures the quantity demanded and Y axis measures the price. DD is the original demand curve where

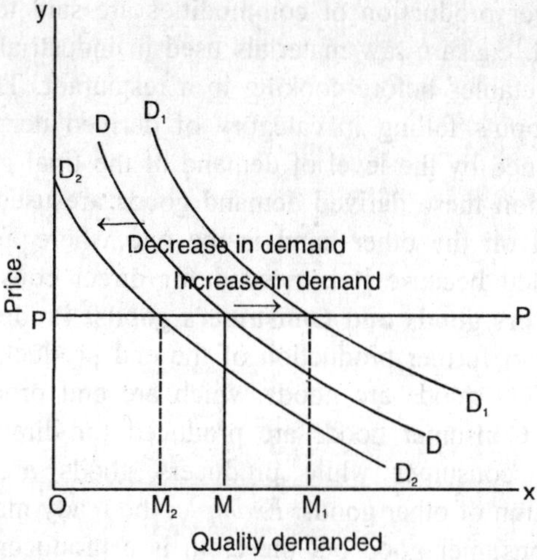

at OP price, OM is the quantity demanded. Given the Op price, which remains constant, when the consumer prefers the commodity, he demands excess of it. Thus due to an increase in demand the demand shift upwards to the new position, which is D_1D_1, and the new demand becomes OM_1. The movement of the demand curve from OM to OM_1 is known as the increase of Demand. On the other hand the price remaining constant, when the consumer does not prefer the commodity, he demands less of it. The demand curve here moves downwards to the new position, which is D_2D_2. This movement of the curve from DD to D_2D_2 is known as the Decrease of demand.

In this analysis, it is seen that the demand of the consumer changes due to interplay of other factors like income, tastes and preference, habits, fashion which can influence the demand for a product apart from the main factor which is price.

3.7. NATURE OF DEMAND — DISTINCTIONS IN DEMAND

Demand for any type of commodity is determined by its nature. Thus it can broadly be classified as:

1. **Derived Demand and Autonomous Demand:** There are certain commodities which are not end products by themselves but which help to become end products in the process of production. Thus those inputs or commodities which are demanded to help

in further production of commodities are said to have derived demand. e.g. are raw materials used in industrial production or the vegetables before cooking in a restaurant. The demand for those inputs falling in category of derived demand is strictly determined by the level of demand of the final goods in whose production these derived demand goods are used. Autonomous demand on the other hand is the one where a commodity is demanded because it is needed for direct consumption.

2. **Producers goods and Consumers goods:** Producers goods are needed in further production of the end product. Where as the consumers goods are goods which are end products in themselves. Consumer goods are produced for direct consumption by the consumer while producers goods are used in the production of other goods. *Example*: the ready made shirt would be a consumer good but the cloth is a producer good, as it is not available for direct use.
3. **Durable and Non-durable goods:** Durable goods can be stored for a longer time and may be put to several uses. The demand for durable will not be frequent as once bought they serve for a longer period of time. The demand for durable goods is elastic in nature. The demand for non-durable goods occurs frequently, as perishable commodities comes under this category. The demand for non-durable is inelastic in nature because though the price changes, they are demanded by consumers because they tend to become necessities of life. *Example* : demand for fruits or cereals is non-durable good and demand for fridge for the same restaurant is a durable good.
4. **Industry and company demand:** The total demand for the products of a particular industry refers to industry demand. Company demand refers to the products of a particular company. An industry covers all firms producing similar products, which are close substitutes, but produced with different brand names. In this aggregate demand of all firms become the industry demand. If the products in the industry are similar or close substitutes we can get industry schedule, which represents the relation of price of the product in the industry with the total quantity of the goods demanded from all the firms in the industry.

5. Short run and long run demand: Demand, which reacts quickly to a change in price is known as short run demand, long run demand on the other hand is the demand which exist after enough time is allowed for the market to adjust itself to new situations. Thus according to Joel Dean, "short run demand refers to demand with its immediate reaction to price changes, income fluctuations, etc., whereas long run demand is that which will ultimately exist as a result of the changes in pricing, promotion or product improvement, after enough time is allowed to let the market adjust itself to the new situation". The short term fluctuations in demand depend upon dome strategic variables like general business activity, income level, price differentials, the seasonal needs etc., on the other hand long term depends upon factors like changes in tastes, technology and life style etc., while factors which were important for short term fluctuations become less and less important in the long run.

3.8. FORECASTING OF DEMAND

Demand basically results in sales of the produced products which constitute the main source of revenue to business. Thus production and sales planning require forecasts of the market conditions and their relationship to demand. Thus prediction of the future demand for the product is essential for the producer to change his production levels, sales and like wise pricing the product.

Thus demand forecasting refers to future demand of a product under given condition. Though the forecasting of the demand may not be exact at times, it gives an rough idea of the demand for the product in the future. In simple words it is an objective assessment of the future course of demand. Demand forecasting is very popular in industrially advanced countries where demand is the limiting factor.

Demand forecasting can be broadly classified into short-term demand forecasting and long term demand forecasting.

1. Short term demand forecasting: This is limited to short period not exceeding one year. It concerns with policies relating to sales. It helps in taking ad-hoc decisions which can help to promote the product in a short period of time. Short term forecasting helps in arriving at suitable price for the product and in deciding about necessary modifications in advertising and in marketing the product.

2. Long term demand forecasting: The assessment of demand for the product and expansion of production units for a long period of time is referred to long term demand forecasting. Long term forecasting enables to take major strategic business decisions. Long term demand forecasting helps in saving the wastages in material, manhours, machine time, and capacity.

Methods of Demand Forecasting

There are various methods involved in forecasting the demand for the product. The two main methods of classification include:

1. The Survey method
2. The Statistical method.

In the survey method, information is elicited from consumers, and thereby arriving at a idea to forecast the demand for the product. In the statistical method, forecasting is done based on certain statistical tools, which help to find the preceding year's demand of the product and also predict the future demand for the product.

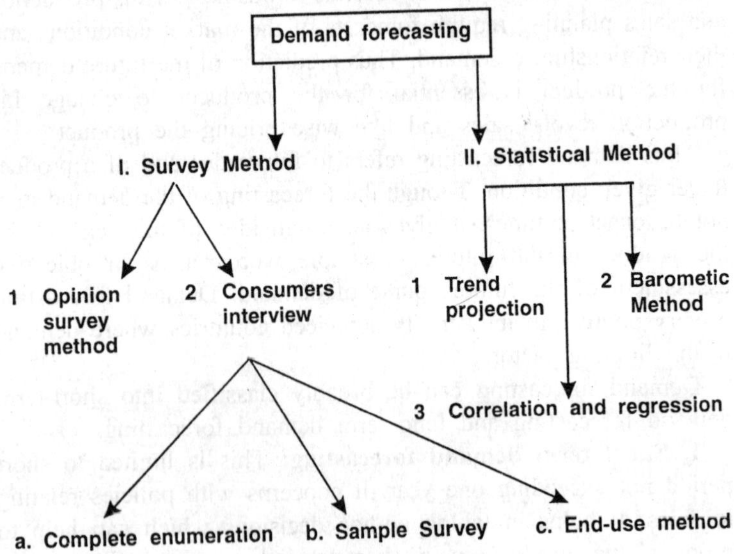

1. Survey Method In this method the demand forecasting for a product is found by conducting a survey with the consumers who use the product. Survey method is divided in to:

I. ***Opinion survey method***: This method is also known as the collective method. According to this method, the expert salesmen are required to estimate the expected sales in their respective areas. These estimates are consolidated and reviewed by the top executives to eliminate the bias in decisions. These are further revised to arrive at a realistic opinion. Thus forecasting is made in this method through the collective wisdom of salesmen, department heads and top executives.

II. ***Consumer survey method***: A sample survey of the consumers is undertaken by interviewing them. Forecasting is done by directly interviewing the consumers and obtaining their views regarding the usage of the product. This approach is partly done based on the attitudes and expectations of the consumers. At times the consumers may be interviewed personally. Or at times they have to answers through questionnaires which are sent to them.

This method is of three types:

a. *Complete enumeration method*: Here an interview of all consumers is conducted. The sum total of individual expected demand for the product gives the demand for the product in the future. However this method is considered more time consuming and tedious.

b. *Sample survey method*: This method is used by taking a sample of consumers for interview. The sampling may be random or stratified sampling. The success in this method depends on making the correct sampling and co-operation of consumers is necessary.

c. *End-use method*: In this method the demand for the end-use of the product and its demand is found separately for the different sectors such as exports, imports, individual industries and consumers. The data obtained through this method helps in manipulating or changing the future course of demand.

2. Statistical Method: Statistical method uses mathematical tools to predict the future demand for a product. This method is used for long term forecasting of the product and also for the product, which already exist in the market.

a. Trend Projection: A firm which is already in the market and which has accumulated data relating to sales during the previous years, would seek to establish the trend in sales for the future years. The past trend is projected in order to interpret the future trend. This type of data is called as trend projection. The time series refers to the data over a period of time. The trend in the time series can be estimated by using: 1. The method of moving averages. 2. The least square method.

1. The Method of Moving Averages

Under this method either a three yearly, or five yearly or seven yearly moving average is calculated. First the moving total based on the said years is calculated, each time giving up the first preceding year from the group. Then it is divided by the number of years in the group. Then the moving average is calculated by dividing the total by the said year which (3,5,or 7) is taken into consideration.

Year	*Demand (in lakhs)*	*3 yearly Moving Total*	*3 yearly Moving Avg.*
1995	10	-	-
1996	15	45	15
1997	20	57	19
1998	22	69	23
1999	27	79	26
2000	30	92	30
2001	35	-	-

the moving average is plotted on a graph and thereby forecasting of a product is obtained.

2. The Method of Least Squares

A firm which has been in existence for a long time would have collected data relating to the sales in the past years. This data will analysed in order to find the trend for the future. The past trend is projected in order to interpret the future trend. The past data is arranged chronologically with regular interval time. This type of trend analysis is termed as time series. The time series on the sales of a product indicates the pattern of its demand under normal conditions.

The time is basically divided into four components:

1. Secular trends—secular trend refers to the changes that occur as a result of general tendency.
2. Seasonal variations—refer to the changes resulting from a change in climate, weather conditions or other which relate to a time period basically a year.
3. Cyclical variations—refers to the changes arising out business fluctuations like a boom period or a depressionary period.
4. Random variations — refers to those which are varied and are unpredictable in nature.

Illustration:

In the time series or trend projection analysis past data of sales are made use of the determine the nature of existing trend, this trend is extrapolated into the future and the rescultant indicated sales are used on the basis.

The sales data of Kiran & Company is given below using the data fit a straight line trend & estimate the sales for 2001.

Year	Sales (Lakhs)	X	X²	XY
1996	240	1	1	240
1997	280	2	4	560
1998	300	3	9	900
1999	280	4	16	1120
2000	340	5	25	1700
n=5	Σy=1440	Σx²=15	Σx²=55	Σxy=4520

Taking Normal equations :

$\Sigma y \;=\; n - a + b\Sigma x$ .... (1)

$\Sigma xy \;=\; ax + b\Sigma x^2$ .... (2)

Substituting values

$1440 = \;\; 5a + 15b$ .... (3)

$4520 = \;\; 15a + 55b$ .... (4)

To solve them equation (3) is multiplied by 3

$$\begin{array}{rcll} & (-) & (-) \quad (-) & \\ \therefore 4320 & = & 15a + 45b & \text{.........................(5)} \\ 4520 & = & 15a + 55b & \text{.........................(6)} \\ \hline 200 & = & 10b & \end{array}$$

$$b = \frac{200}{10} = 20$$

Substituting values of be is equation 3

$$1440 = 5a + 300$$

$$= 5a = 1440 - 300;\ 5a = 1140;$$

$$= 5a = 1140$$

$$a = \frac{1140}{5}$$

$$= 228$$

Now using the straight line equation $y = a + bx$
We obtain the trend values for the preceding and also for the future years.

1996 = 228 + 20 (1) = 248
1997 = 228 + 20 (2) = 268
1998 = 228 + 20 (3) = 288
1999 = 228 + 20 (4) = 308
2000 = 228 + 20 (5) = 328

To obtain the trend for 2001
2001 = 228 + 20(6) = 348 lakhs

These data of sales for five years are plotted as a graph, the value of sales on the 'y' axis and the year on the x axis. The trend line for this particular data shows an increasing trend.

The trend line is fitted by developing an equation giving the nature and magnitude of the trend. The common method of constructing the line of best fit is by the method of least squares.

The same analysis is also used in the hotel industry to analyse the flow of guest (or to analyse during and department in the hotel period of time a year for instance let us assume). In predicting the number of guest arrivals in Hotel Kanishk for the year 2002. The data of the preceding years, let us say from 1997 is analysed. This data shows that the tourist numbers has increased gradually by each year. This increasing trend also helps the properietor to

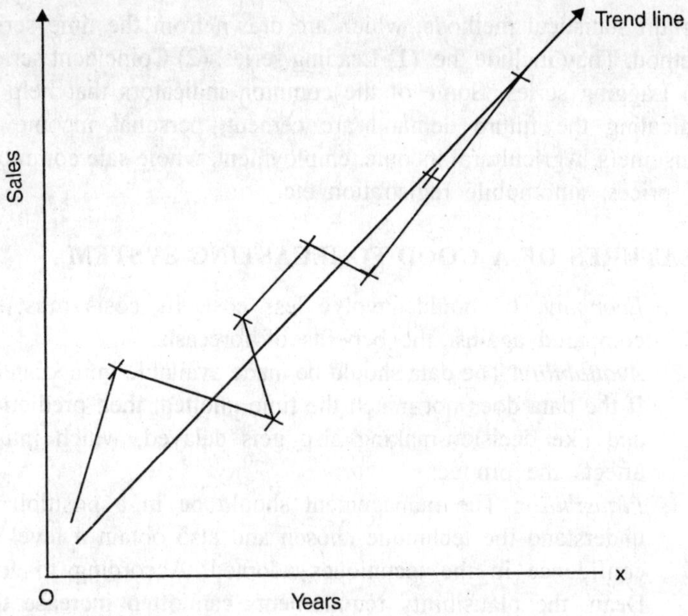

forecast an increasing number of tourist for the Year 2002, than the previous years.

3. Regression and Correlation Method

By this method the nature and extent of relationship between the variables by means of statistical and econometric techniques. In this method relationship between variables is determined which help aid in forecast. A regression equation is obtained to show the relationship between sales and several independent variables. The aim is to separate the variables and measure the relation between variations in sales and the corresponding changes in the principal determinants of demand. The results obtained from the regression and correlation analysis is also referred to as economic model building.

4. Economic Indicators

This method is also known as the Barometric method. In this method the events, which have occurred in the present, are used to predict the directions of change in the future. This is done by certain statistical methods, which are drawn from the time series method. They include the: (1) Leading series. (2) Coincident series. (3) Lagging series. Some of the common indicators that help in indicating the future demand are cement, personal income of consumers. Agricultural income, employment, whole sale commodity prices, automobile registration etc.

FEATURES OF A GOOD FORECASTING SYSTEM

1. *Economy*: It should involve less cost. Its costs must be compared against the benefits of forecasts.
2. *Availability*: The data should be made available immediately. If the data does not match the time allotted, then prediction and like decision-making also gets delayed, which inturn affects the product.
3. *Plausibility*: The management should be in a position to understand the technique chosen and also obtain a level of confidence in the techniques adopted. According to Joel Dean, the plausibility requirements can often increase the accuracy of the result.
4. *Simplicity*: The method adopted must be simple in nature. Complicated mathematical and econometric techniques makes forecasting a tedious procedure, which inturn delays the decision making process.
5. *Accuracy*: Forecast should be accurate as far as possible, is accuracy must be judged by examining the past forecasts I the light of the present situation.

MODEL QUESTIONS

Short Questions

1. Give a market demand schedule.
2. What are consumer goods?
3. Given an example of short run demand.
4. Differenciate between derived and autonomous demand.
5. Explain the term economic indicators.
6. Explain the term barometric method.
7. Explain the main features of a good forcasting method in the hotel industry.
8. Explain the regression method of forecasting the demand.

9. Doės speculation help in changing the demand for a product? If yes what is type of invovled?
10. What are cyclical variations in demand? How is it different random variation?
11. Differenciate between opinion survey and consumer interview method.
12. Give as example for durable and non-durable goods.
13. Give an example for substitute and complementary goods.
14. Give an example for necessary and luxury goods.
15. Give an example to explain the analysis increase and decrease of demand.

4

Elasticity of Demand

4.1. MEANING

The chapter on demand analyses the reaction of the demand of the consumer with regard to changes in the price of the commodity. It states the movement of demand upward or drawnward due to change in price. It does not know to what extent the demand changes, but the elasticity analyses the extent of changes in the demand for the commodity due to a change in the price of the commodity.

It was Alfred Marshall who introduced the concept of elasticity of demand for the first time. Elasticity of demand measures the responsiveness of change in demand due to change in the price of the commodity. For Example if the price of ice-cream falls, people would demand it more than it was demanded before. Thus According to Stonier and Hague, "Elasticity of demand is therefore a technical term used by the economists to describe the degree of responsiveness of the demand for a commodity to a fall in its price". The elasticity of demand has also been referred to, as the price elasticity of demand. Elasticity of demand measures the change in demand of the consumer when he is demanding the goods, due to the change in price.

The elasticity has been broadly classified as elastic demand and inelastic demand depending on its intensity.

1. **Elastic Demand.** When the responsiveness of the change in demand is greater than the responsiveness of the change in price it is known as the elastic demand. For example, Raju is demanding 12 kg of tea in a month, when the price of rice is Rs. 18 per kg. Now for instance if the price of

rice increases to Rs. 25, then Raju would demand only 8 kg. it is thus seen that the demand for commodity decreases more drastically than the increase in its price.

2. **Inelastic Demand.** When the responsiveness of the change in demand is less than the responsiveness of the change in price, it is known as inelastic demand. For example, Surya is demanding 2 kg of tomatoes per week when the price is Rs. 12, now for instance if the price of tomatoes falls to Rs. 7 per kg. Surya would only increase her buying from 2 to 3 kg.

The elasticity of demand may be classified into three types depending on the main factors influencing the demand for the commodity:

1. Price elasticity of demand
2. Income elasticity of demand
3. Cross elasticity of demand

4.2.1. PRICE ELASTICITY OF DEMAND

When the responsiveness of change in demand is due to the change in price, it is referred to as price elasticity of demand. The price elasticity of demand may thus, be defined as the ratio of the relative change in price. The co-efficient of price elasticity is therefore measured as:

$$E_d = \frac{\textbf{Percentage change in the quantity demanded}}{\textbf{Percentage change in the price}}$$

Or

$$E_d = \frac{\textbf{Proportionate change in the quantity demanded}}{\textbf{Proportionate change in price}}$$

The price elasticity of demand shows the extent of response of demand for a commodity to a given change in price, other demand determinants remaining constant. It can also be algebraically be written as

$$e = \frac{\Delta Q}{\Delta P} \times \frac{P}{Q}$$

Where Q = Original demand
P = Original price
ΔQ = Change in demand
ΔP = Change in price

Eg. When the price of rice is Rs. 100, person Z was demanding 35 kg Now, when the price is increased to Rs. 12, he demands only 25 kg the price elasticity is

$$e = \frac{\Delta Q}{\Delta P} \times \frac{P}{Q}$$

$$= \frac{10}{2} \times \frac{10}{35}$$

$$= 1.4$$

Types of Price Elasticity of Demand

The different types of price elasticity of demand are:

1. Relatively elastic demand
2. Relatively inelastic demand
3. Unitary elastic demand
4. Perfectly elastic demand
5. Perfectly inelastic demand

1. **Relatively elastic demand:** When the proportion of change in quantity demanded is greater than that of price, the demand is said to be relatively elastic. The value of elasticity is greater

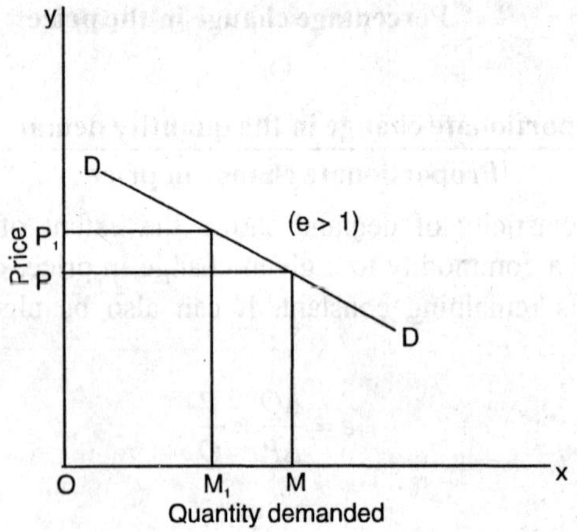

than one in this case — E >1. For example, the price of wheat is 10 per kg and the consumer is demanding 15 kg of wheat. If for instance the price of wheat increases to Rs. 12 per kg the consumer demands only 9 kg, the price elasticity of demand is 2. Hence the value of elasticity if demand is greater than one.

The shape of relatively elastic demand curve is a flatter curve. In the above figure DD is the demand curve which slopes downwards. OP is the price is the price at OM is quantity demanded. When the price increases to slightly to OP1, the demand falls to OM1. Here the fall in demand is said to be drastic.

2. **Relatively inelastic demand:** When the demand for a commodity shows a small response to a greater change in price, it is known as relatively elastic demand. That is when the proportion of change in demand is less that the proportion of change in price, it is known as relatively inelastic demand. For example if consumer Z is buying 50 units of the commodity at Rs. 25 per commodity, now if the price decreases to Rs. 20 per unit. Consumer Z would only slightly increases his buying from 52 units. The elasticity of demand here is 0.2, which is less than one and hence the elasticity is said to be relatively elastic.

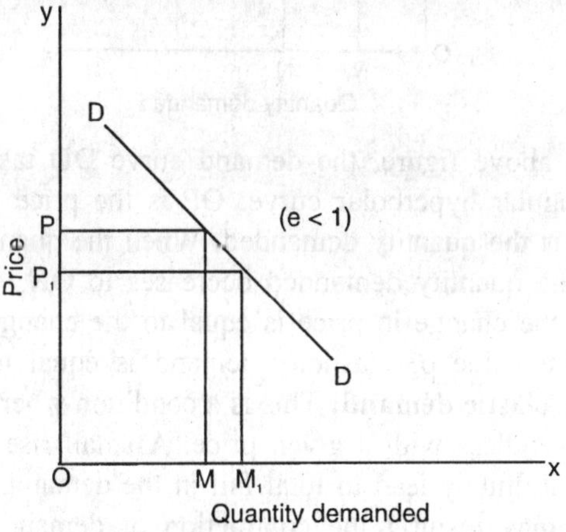

In the above figure, the shape of the demand curve is a steeper demand curve. DD is the demand curve. On the Y axis the price is measured and on the X axis Quantity demanded is measured. OP is the price at the OM is the Quantity demanded. When the Price falls to OP_1, the quantity demanded increases slightly to OM_1. The distance between the change in the price and distance between the change in the demand shows that the value of elasticity is less than one — E<1.

3. **Unitary elastic demand:** when the proportionate change in the quantity is equal to the proportionate change in the price, it is known as unitary elastic demand. For example, if the proportionate increase in the price of the commodity is 25 per cent. The proportionate decrease in the demand for the commodity is 25 per cent and not more than it. The value of elasticity here is exactly equal to one.

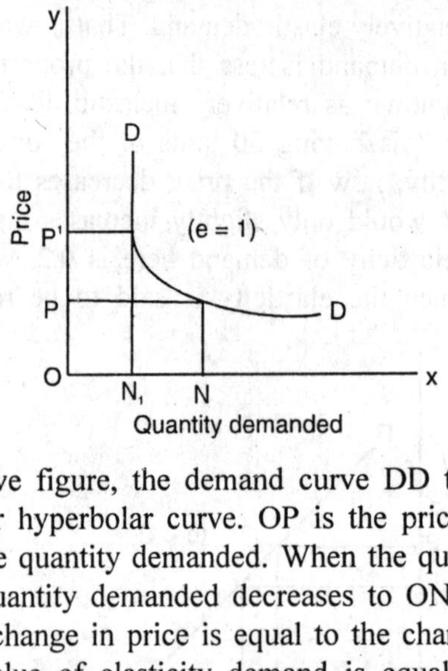

In the above figure, the demand curve DD takes the shape of rectangular hyperbolar curve. OP is the price at ON is the quantity is the quantity demanded. When the quantity increases to OP_1 the quantity demanded decreases to ON_1. The distance between the change in price is equal to the change in demand. Hence the value of elasticity demand is equal to one, E=1.

4. **Perfectly elastic demand:** This is a condition where the demand becomes endless with a given price. A small rise in price will result in infinitely lead to total fall in the demand. A small rise in price may result I the contraction of demand to zero and small drop in price may result in extension of demand. The numerical coefficient of perfectly elastic demand is equal to infinity.

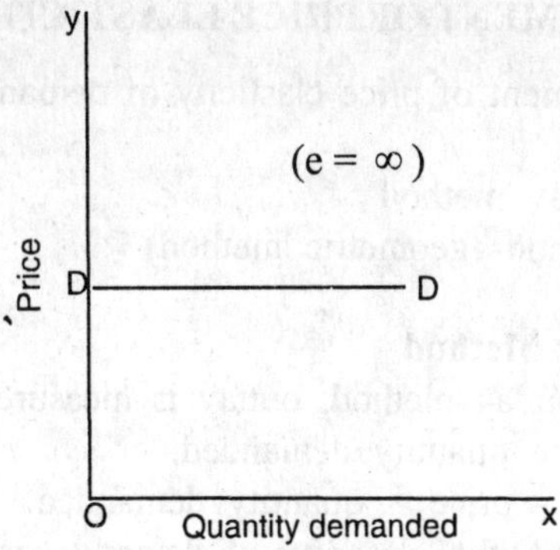

5. Perfectly inelastic demand: When the demand for a commodity shows no response to a change in price, it is called perfectly inelastic demand. Even a large fall in price will not induce the quantity of demand to be more, nor a large rise in the price will prevent the consumers from buying less. The value of elasticity of demand is equal to 0.

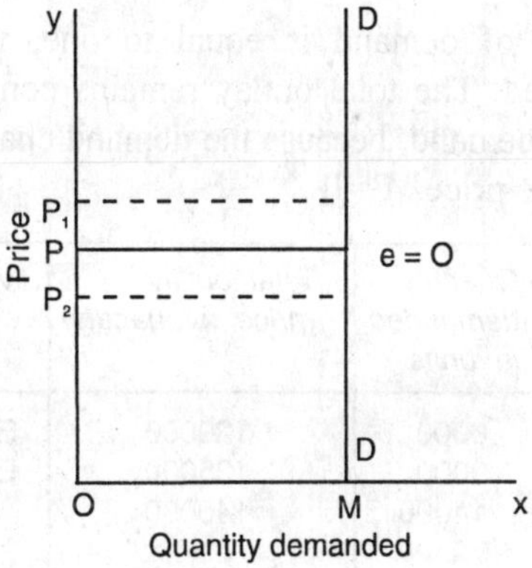

In the Figure, DD is the demand curve which takes the shape of a vertical straight line which is parallel to Y axis. At the given price OP, the quantity demanded is OM. Now if the price increases to OP_1 the demand remains still at OM. Even if the price of the commodity decreases to OP_2, the quantity remains still at OM. Since the demand does not show any response to the change in the price of the commodity, the value of elasticity becomes zero.

4.3. MEASUREMENT OF PRICE ELASTICITY OF DEMAND

The measurement of price elasticity of demand can be done in two ways:

1. Total outlay method
2. Point method (geometric method)

1. Total Outlay Method

In the total outlay method, outlay is measured by multiplying the price and the quantity demanded.

Total outlay = price × quantity demanded.

In this method, the elasticity of demand can be measured in three ways. The elasticity is greater than one, when with increase in price the total outlay decreases, and with an decrease in price, the total outlay increases. This is when E > 1.

Elasticity of demand is less than one, when with an increase in price the total outlay increases, and with a fall in price the total outlay decreases. This is when the value of elasticity is less than one E<1.

The Elasticity of demand is equal to one, when the outlay remains unchanged. The total outlay remains constant in the case of unitary elastic demand, because the demand changes in the same proportion as the price. E=1.

Price in Rs	*Quantity demanded in units*	*Total outlay (price x quantity)*	*Value of elasticity*
I. Rs 20.00	6000	120000	Elastic demand E > 1
Rs 15.00	9000	135000	
Rs 10.00	14000	140000	
II. Rs 20.00	6000	120000	Inelastic demand E < 1
Rs 15.00	7000	105000	
Rs 10.00	8000	80000	
III. Rs 20.00	6000	120000	Unitary Elastic demand E = 1.
Rs 15.00	8000	120000	
Rs 10.00	12000	120000	

The total outlay method is explained through a table. In the first case when the demand is elastic, it is seen that when the price is Rs. 15 the outlay is 135000 and when the price increases to Rs. 20 the outlay falls to 120000. For instance if the price falls to Rs. 10 the outlay increases to 140000. This shows the inverse relationship between price and quantity demanded, i.e., when the price is high outlay is less and when falls the outlay increases.

In the second case, the demand is inelastic, when the price is Rs. 15 the total outlay is 105000, when the price increases to Rs. 20 the outlay increases to 120000. And when the price falls to Rs. to 10 the outlay falls to 80000. It thus shows price and outlay are directly related to one another. This is when the demand in elastic in nature.

In the third case the demand is equal to one. When the price Rs. 15 the outlay is 120000. When the price increases to Rs. 20, the outlay is 120000, the outlay remains the same. Similarly, when the price falls to Rs. 10, the outlay still remains the same at 120000. This is because a little more is demanded, hence the outlay remains constant it is thus seen that when the price changes the demand get itself adjusted either by increasing or decreasing thereby keeping the total outlay constant. Here the value of E = 1.

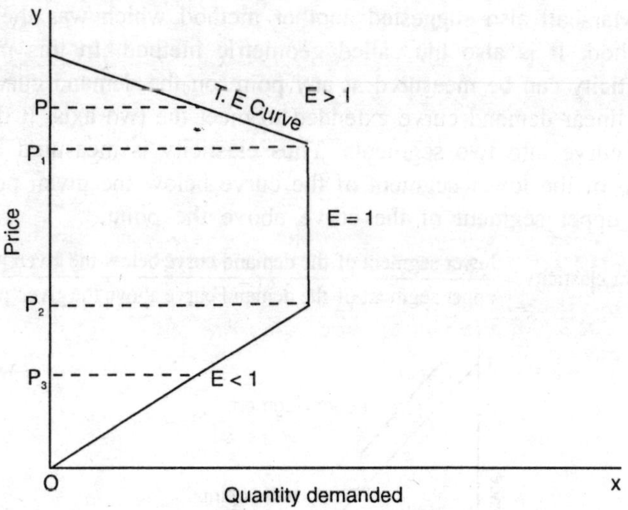

The total outlay method can also explained through a figure. In the figure price is measured on the Y axis and on the X axis quantity demanded is measured. OP to OP_1, OP_1 to OP_2, OP_2 to

OP_3 are considered different price ranges. The total out lay curve curves slopes downwards indicating the fall in price with and the total outlay increasing. With a increase in price from OP_1 to OP total expenditure decreases as shown by the curve sloping to the left. So the demand a this price range is elastic and E is greater than 1. When the price is Between OP_2 and OP_3 the total expenditure curve shows that as the price falls the expenditure increases showing that the demand is inelastic and E is less than 1. In the price range P_1P_2 the total expenditure does not change. The fall in price or rise in price keeps the total outlay constant as this part of the curve remains vertical to Y axis showing the total amount being constant. Hence the elasticity is unity. Thus in the total outlay method elasticity can be measured in three ways $E > 1$, $E < 1$, $E = 1$.

The main draw back of this method is that the exact value of elasticity cannot be found out.

2. Point Method

Marshall also suggested another method which was the point method. It is also the called geometric method. In this method elasticity can be measured at any point on the demand curve. On the linear demand curve extended to meet the two axis. It divides the curve into two segments. Thus elasticity is measured by the ratio of the lower segment of the curve below the given point to the upper segment of the curve above the point.

$$\text{Point elasticity} = \frac{\text{lower segment of the demand curve below the given point}}{\text{upper segment of the demand curve above the given point.}}$$

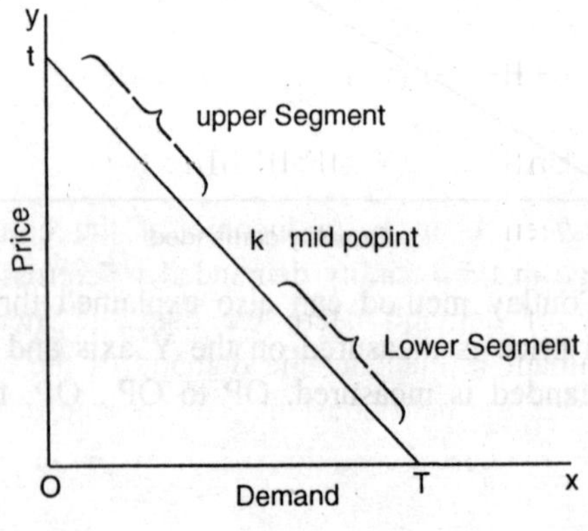

In the figure elasticity at point $K = \frac{KT}{Kt}$

In order to find out the elasticity of demand at any point on the demand curve a tangent line to that point in the demand curve is drawn so that the tangent may cut axis on both sides X and Y. Elasticity of demand can be calculated by finding the length of upper segment and the lower segment.

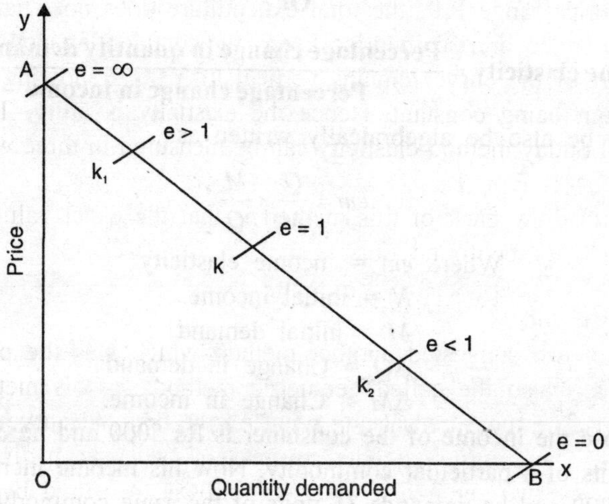

AB is the demand curve, where k is the mid point, which devides the lower and upper segment. At point k, e = 1

Between k & k_1 e > 1

Between k1 & A = e = ∞

Between k & K_2 = e < 1

Between k2 & B = 0

4.4. INCOME ELASTICITY OF DEMAND

The relation between changes in income of the consumer and consequent change in the quantity demanded is expressed through income elasticity of demand. Here we take the income as an important determinant influencing the demand of the commodity. All the other factors are held constant. The income elasticity thus tries to find the effect of a increase or decrease in income and consequent change in demand. Income elasticity of demand is the ratio of proportionate change in the quantity demanded of a commodity to a given proportionate change in the income of the consumer. According to Stonier and Hague, "Income elasticity shows the responsiveness of a consumer's purchases of a particular good to a change in his income".

$$\textbf{Income elasticity} = \frac{\textbf{Percentage change in quantity demanded}}{\textbf{Percentage change in income}}$$

Or

$$\textbf{Income elasticity} = \frac{\textbf{Percentage change in quantity demanded}}{\textbf{Percentage change in income}}$$

It can be also be algebraically written as

$$em = \frac{Q}{M} \times \frac{M}{Q}$$

Where em = income elasticity
N = initial income.
M = initial demand
ΔQ = Change in demand
ΔM = Change in income.

Suppose the income of the consumer is Rs 5000 and he demands 25 units of a particular commodity. Now his income increases to Rs. 7000 and he demands 35 units of the same commodity. Here the income elasticity $= \frac{10}{2000} \times \frac{5000}{25} = 1$ income elasticity is one.

4.5. CROSS ELASTICITY OF DEMAND

Cross elasticity explains the proportionate change in demand of say commodity x due to proportionate change in price of commodity y. Which may either be a substitute good or complementary good.

$$\textbf{Cross elasticity of commodity x} = \frac{\textbf{Proportionate change in demand of commodity x}}{\textbf{Proportionate change in price of commodity y}}$$

It can also algebraically written as

$$exy = \frac{\Delta Qx}{\Delta Py} \times \frac{Py}{Qx}$$

Where e_{xy} = Cross elasticity of demand for substitute commodities x and y.

Qx = Initital quantity demanded of commodity x

Py = Initial price of commodity y.

ΔQx = Change in quantity demanded of commodity x

ΔPy = Change in price of commodity y.

4.6. FACTORS INFLUENCING THE ELASTICITY OF DEMAND

There are various factors which effect the elasticity of a commodity:

1. Nature of the commodity: Goods are classified into necessities and luxury commodities based on their usage. The demand for necessities like rice, wheat, etc., will be inelastic in nature. What ever be the price for these commodities, they would be demanded, as are essential commodities. On the other hand the demand for comforts and luxuries like cars, fridge etc., will fall rapidly when there is a slight increase in their prices. The demand is elastic here. Thus, the elasticity of demand varies depending on the type of the commodity.

2. Use of the commodity: If the commodity is frequently used its demand becomes inelastic in nature. If the commodity has less usage its elasticity becomes high. When the commodity is put to various uses, it will have elastic demand even if the price of that commodity is increased, the commodity will be demanded extensively. For example railways and households use coal. But the former's demand is inelastic while the latter's demand is elastic. Thus the demand for a multi-use commodity in those uses where marginal utility is high will be inelastic while in those uses where the marginal utility is low, the demand will be elastic.

3. Substitutes: Commodities having substitutes have elastic demand, and those without substitutes have inelastic demand. When the price of a commodity rises, the consumers would shift their preference to a substitute commodity whose price is less. For example a rise in the price of rice would force the consumers to buy more its substitute commodity that is wheat. The demand is elastic in this case.

On the other hand if the commodity has no substitutes, even at a higher price, consumers would be force to buy the commodity rather than going without it. For instance let us assume consumers want warm clothing in winter, even at prices they would buy them.

4. Habits: If the consumers are addicted to some habits and customs, then the demand of the commodity will be inelastic. For instance if some consumers are addicted to a particular brand of clothing, they would not change their demand, even if the price of this commodity increased.

5. Money spent: Elasticity of demand for a commodity also depends on the proportion of consumers money spent on the commodity. If the consumer spends a small consumption the demand for that commodity will be inelastic. In case of food, clothing the consumers spend a large proportion of income and therefore any increase in price will result in sizeably increasing his total expenditure. Thus the demand for these commodities will be elastic.

6. Demand: There are certain commodities, which are frequently demanded by consumers. The demand is inelastic in those cases. For example in case of necessity items like food, shelter, the demand is inelastic in these cases, this is because even if there is increase in the prices of these commodities they will have to be used. There are certain types of goods whose demand can be postponed. This can happen in case of luxury commodities, when with the increase of these commodities, there is a fall in demand. Consumers do purchase them at higher prices. Hence demand is said to be elastic in luxury goods whose demand can be postponed.

7. Time Factor: Demand for a particular commodity exists for a day, week, month or for years. Thus it is seen that the demand is inelastic during the short period. It will be comparatively elastic in the long run. For example if the consumer is using a particular brand of clothing, in the short period if the price of this clothing increases, the consumer demands the same item, because in the short period of time he cannot decide to shift to another commodity. In the long run he may have better chances of shifting to a better brand whose price is also less. The elasticity of demand is inelastic in this case.

The analysis of demand helps in understanding the needs and

preference of consumers. The hotel industry though a service sector is considered to be an industry, which works to provide various kinds of services to its guests. The concept of demand here will help in understanding the needs of the guests, whether it is in the form of providing the different types of accommodation, food, etc. Forecasting the demand in the hotel industry can be related to the flow of customers to a restaurant or a hotel and their demand. Here an analysis can be made on the number of visitors, their various demands over a period of time-the increasing or the decreasing trend and thereby to forecast the needed changes in the future. Elasticity of demand indicates how these factors which can influence the demand for a commodity, the nature of demand being elastic or inelastic in nature.

MODEL QUESTIONS

Short Questions

1. Explain the law of demand.
2. What is giffen paradox?
3. State the difference between extension of demand and increase of demand.
4. What do you mean by demand forecasting?
5. Explain Veblen effect.
6. Differenciate between necessary & luxury goods.

Essay Questions

1. Explain the law of demand and it demerits.
2. Explain the different price elasticities of demand.
3. Explain the various methods of analysing demand forecasting.
4. What are the various factors that determine the elasticity of demand for a commodity?

5
Production Function

5.1. MEANING

Production is an activity that creates utility or value. It includes the process where the raw material is converted into a finished product. This transformation process can take three dimensions: change in form, space and time. Thus the production theory is applicable not only to the production, distribution and storage of tangible goods, but also applies to service activities. In the hotel or a restaurant also there may be different areas-the food and beverage department, the front office, the service department and the others, which act as one unit in servicing the customers. Taking the food and beverage department — the main function of this department is to provide food of different kinds. To produce the final output that is 'food' of whatever kind there is the activity of converting the raw material to final product. This activity is also called production.

The production function is a purely technical relationship, which connects factor inputs and output. Stigler states, "The production function is the name given to the relationship between rates of input of productive services and the rate of output of product". It can also be defined as the functional relationship under the given technology, between physical rates of input and output of a firm, per unit of time. In simple words it may be stated as, "technical relationship that exists between input and output is termed as production function."

In algebraic terms it may written as:

$$Q = f(a, b, c, d, \ldots\ldots n, \overline{T})$$

Where Q represents the physical quantity of output.
f denotes the functional relationship
a, b, c, d, n represent the quantities of various inputs
T refers to the prevailing technology
(–) bar on the top of T indicates the technology to be constant.

It can also be expressed Qx = f (K, L)

Where Qx represents the output of the commodity
f denotes the functional relationship
K refers to the capital
L refers to labour.

5.2. FEATURES RELATED TO PRODUCTION FUNCTION

State of Technology It relates to the state of technology involved in the production process. The effect of technology whether it is updated or out dated technology can reflect itself in the final out put of the product.

Flow Concept Production relates to the flow of inputs and the resulting flow of output of a commodity during a period of time. Here time plays an important role.

Inputs Refers to those factors such as raw materials which go into the production process. The basic factors include land, labour, capital, organization.

Short run and the long run production function

The functional relationship which exists between the input and output depends on the time element to a large extent. There can be production, which can exist only for a short period and one which can last for a longer period of time.

Short Run Period: The term 'short run' is defined as a period of time, which can last for a fortnight a month or a couple of months. This is period of time where the inputs of factors of production cannot be changed totally. There are certain factors like land, equipment, which are expensive in nature. These factors cannot be varied in a short period of time.

Long Run Period: The 'long run' is a period of time which can last for long period of time, and where necessary changes can be made not only in variable factor but also in the fixed factors. Thus there is no distinction between fixed and variable factors in the long run, as all factors are variable in the short period of time. The long run is related to operational time involved in altering the fixed factors. The duration of the production varies between different industries. *For example*: to establish a restaurant one needs land, building, equipments, labour etc. After a few months or a year due to high flow of customers to the restaurant, if the proprietor wants to expand the restaurant, he can do so, because the time taken is sufficient enough to expand the existing place. This may not be possible in the short run period, if required the proprietor can only intensively use the existing plant.

FACTORS INVOLVED IN THE PRODUCTION PROCESS

The factors of production acts as important components for converting the raw material in to the finished product. The factors are basically divided into the fixed and variable factors.

Fixed Factors: Fixed factors are those factors on which the investment is too high. They cannot be changed in the short period of time and can be varied only in the long run period. Example land, heavy equipment, plant.

Variable Factors: Refers to those factors which can be changed during the short period. They are factors on which the investment rate is quite less. *Example*: investment on labour, raw material etc.

LAWS OF PRODUCTION

The production process involves the transformation of all inputs into output. During the process of production various combinations of inputs are used to obtain an output. Thus the production function traces a relationship between the various combinations of input and output. The classical economists tried to use the returns from agriculture to explain the law of returns.

Law of increasing returns: According to Joan Robinson, "When an increased amount of any factor of production is devoted to certain use. It is often the case that improvement in organization can be introduced which will make natural units of factor more efficient, so that there is an increase in output". The law of increasing returns refers to a situation where in the combination of input leads, to greater proportionate increase in output.

Law of constant returns: According to Prof Stigler, "When all the productive services are increased in a given proportion, the out put is increased in same proportion". In other words, it refers to a situation where in the total output increases exactly in proportion to increase in the factors of production induced in to production system.

Law of diminishing returns: According to Marshall, "An increase in capital and labour applied in the cultivation of land causes in general a less than proportionate increase in the amount of produce raised, unless it happens to coincide with an improvement in the art of agriculture". In the initial stages of cultivation on a given piece of land, when additional units of capital and labour are invested additional output may be more proportionate, but after a certain extent when the land is cultivated with some more investment, the additional output will be less than proportionate under given circumstances, unless some improvements take place in the techniques of cultivation.

5.3. LAW OF VARIABLE PROPORTION

Production is the back bone of all economic activity. The main objective of every producer is to maximize his profits with the given input. In the process the producer combines various inputs to get a suitable output, thus varying certain inputs and keeping the other factors of input constant. The level of output of a firm depends on the combination of different factors of production viz., land, labour, capital and organization. An increase in production would be possible when either the quantity of all the factors is increased simultaneously or when the quantity of some of the factors is increased. Thus the law of variable proportion states that, 'As the proportion of one factor in a combination of factors is increased after a point, the average and marginal production of factor will diminish'. Professor Stigler defines it as, "Equal increments of one input are added, the inputs of other productive services being held constant, beyond a certain point. The resulting increments of product will decrease i.e., the marginal product will diminish".

Thus in the short run, as the amount of variable factor increases, other things remaining equal, the output will increase more than proportionately to the amount of variable inputs in the beginning, that it may increase in the same proportion and ultimately it will increase less proportionately.

Certain concepts have to be known to understand the law of variable proportion:

- ***Total Product (TP)***: It refers to the total units of out put produced per unit of time by combining the inputs. In the short run however, the total product increases with an increase in the variable factor.

  Thus TP = f(QVF),

  where TP denotes total produce

  QVF denotes the quantity of the variable factor

  Example: 30 workers produce 40 shirts in a day. Here the total product is 40 units.

- ***Average Product***: Refers to the product per unit of product. In other words it is obtained by dividing the total product by the quantity of the product produced.

$$\mathbf{AP = \frac{TP}{QVF}}$$

  Suppose, 5 units of the labour gives out 100 units of the product. Here the average product is 100 / 5 = 20 units. Hence 20 units is the average product.

- ***Marginal Product***: The additional product obtained due to the additional input induced into the production system is known is marginal product. The marginal concept plays an important in the production system, as the producer is keen to known the additional product produced and the additional profit obtained thereon. Algebraically, it may written as $MP_n = TP_n - TP_{n-1}$. Suppose, 20 workers produce 100 units of the commodity in a day. And the next day an additional 2 workers are employed and the production is 120 units. The marginal product is 20 units.

ASSUMPTIONS

- The state of technology remains constant and unchanged, if for instance the technology changes the average and marginal output will increase and not decrease.
- The fixed factors are kept constant and the variable factors are changed due to increase in the level of output.
- All units of variable factors are homogenous.
- The entire operation is only for the short run and not for the long run period.

The law of variable proportion can be explained through the table below:

Variable Factor	*Total Product*	*Average Product(TP/N)*	*Marginal Product (MP) ($TP_n - TP_{n-1}$)*	
1	10	10	10	Stage I
2	25	12.5	15	
3	45	15	20	
4	70	17.5	25	Stage II
5	88	17.6	18	
6	100	16.7	12	
7	107	15.3	7	
8	107	13.4	0	Stage III
9	106	11.8	–1	
10	102	10.2	–4	

In the schedule it is seen that as the doses of the variable factor is induced into the production system, the total product, the average product, and the marginal product keep increasing in the first stage. As the doses of the variable factor is further induced into the production system, it is seen that the total product increases, but at a diminishing rate, the average product also decreases, but the rapid changes are noticed in the marginal product, where its value diminishes more than the decrease in the average product. This stage is also known as stage of decreasing returns. When the doses of variable factor are further added to the production system, the total product and average product diminish further. The marginal product diminishes reaches a zero level and then a negative level. It can also be seen that the when the marginal is zero, the total product is maximum. Even after this point, if the variable factor

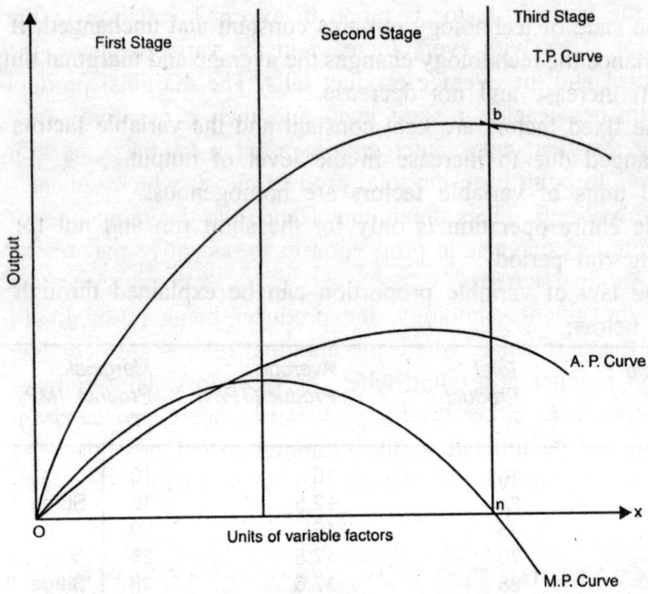

is added, the total product only shows a decline in production.

The law of variable proportion can also be explained through a figure.

In the figure x axis measures the units of variable factor. And y axis measures the output. In the first stage, the total product, the average product and the marginal product curve increase, with an increase in every additional input. This stage is known as stage of increasing returns. When the short run production function is adjusted to obtain the maximum output, the resulting output tends to be in a greater proportionate to the increase in the variable factor units. The services of certain factors like that of the machines will be used more efficiently when greater input of variable factors like labour and raw material are applied.

In the second stage, the increasing dosage of input results in diminishing returns to scale. In the short period, since the fixed factors cannot be changed, the firm seeks to increase output by employing more and more units of variable factors, thus the imperfect substitution of factors leads to internal diseconomies and thereby diminishing returns to scale.

In the third stage, there is negative returns to scale, where the input of the variable factor is much in excess in relation to the fixed factor. Thus with every increase in the variable factor, the total product and the average product falls. The marginal product also diminishes reaches a zero level and then a negative level. When the marginal curve intercepts at point n on the x axis, it corresponds to point b on the total product curve, which indicates that when MP = 0, TP is maximum. Hence the declining part of the total product curve is in proportion to the negative part of the marginal product curve.

Under the given technology, the producer being rational will not reach the third stage, where the marginal returns are negative, he will not produce at a point, where he faces loss. The producer will not choose to either produce much in stage I, as the fixed factor will not be utilized to the optimum extent possible. The second stage is one in which the producer would tend to use both the factors in order to maximize his profits.

SIGNIFICANCE OF THE LAW

The economic significance of the law is that it is useful to producers in taking appropriate decisions with regard to the type of commodity to be produced and if needed to take adhoc decision to diversify into a new product region, or to produce an entirely new product. Given the variation in the total output and marginal out put, it helps the producer to find the appropriate region which would enable him to produce to the optimum and thereby earn profits.

5.4. ISOQUANT CURVES

Isoquant curves represent all those possible combinations of inputs which produce the same level of output. Isoquants have a negative slope, isoquants curves are convex to the origin. Which indicates that in order to maintain a given level of output, the quantity of one factor of input to that of another should either increase or decrease.

In other words the isoquant slope measures the rate of technical substitution of one factor input for the other factor input.

The slope of the isoquant curve measures the rate of technical substitution of one factor input to that of another factor input.

$$MRTS_{LC} = \frac{\Delta C}{\Delta L}$$

Where ΔC = change in capital
ΔL = change in labour

Isoquants indicate that in the long run all inputs are variable. In the following table the isoquant technique is explained.

Combination	Labour	Machinery	Output
A	8	2	50 units
B	6	4	50 units
C	5	5	50 units
D	3	8	50 units

Here there are two factor inputs, namely labour and machinery. It shows how the different combination of labour and machinery can produce same level of output. For example in the combination, 8 units of labour and 2 machinery are induced to produce 50 units of output. And in the second combination B, 6 units of labour and 4 units machinery are induced to produce 50 units of output. In combination C 5 units of labour and 5 units of machinery are induced to obtain the same level of output. In the combination D 3 units of labour and 8 units of machinery are induced to obtain the same level of output. The above table indicates that the change in the combination, is capable of producing the same level of output.

Optimum factor Combination : The optimum factor examines how the producer combines the various factor inputs to the optimum level, in order to obtain the maximum output and like wise maximise his profits.

A rational producer tries to maximize his profits, and he also tries to combine the factors inputs in such a way, which involves the least cost of production and in which the return fetches maximum returns. In determining the optimum or least cost combination, the producer is guided by the principle of equi-marginal returns, which is based on the law of substitution. The firm obtains maximum returns or equilibrium when the last unit of money spent yields the same amount of marginal returns.

If the marginal return of labour exceeds the marginal returns of capital it will substitute labour for capital till the marginal returns of both the factors become equal. Thus the least cost combination may be stated as:

$$\frac{\textbf{Marginal productivity of Labour}}{\textbf{Price of Labour}} = \frac{\textbf{Marginal productivity of capital}}{\textbf{Price of capital}}$$

In symbolic terms : $\frac{MPL}{PL} > \frac{MPC}{PC}$

The producer would substitute labour for capital till

$$\frac{MPL}{PL} > \frac{MPC}{PC}$$

Isocost Curves

Isocost curves shows the various combinations of two factors of production which a producer can obtain with a given outlay. These curves help the producer in obtaining the maximum benefits with a fixed money outlay. The isocost curve is explained through a figure.

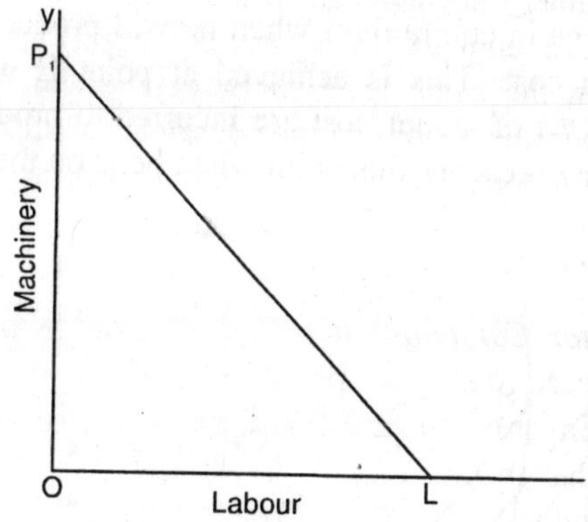

A producer has Rs. 4000 to buy two factors namely labour and machinery. If the price of labour is Rs 10, the producer employs 200 labourers and pays Rs. 2000. If the cost of machinery is Rs. 1000, he buys 2 machines. Thus in the figure, P_1 shows 200 labourers and L_1 shows that 2 machines can be bought with Rs. 4000. By connecting the points P_1L_1, we obtain what is called the isocost line.

5.5. EQUILIBRIUM POINT IN THE PRODUCTION PROCESS

A producer is in equilibrium when he is producing the derived output at the least possible cost. An iso product map shows a set of iso product curves which indicate the different combinations of the factors of production each of which can produce a specifies the level of output.

On the other hand, an isocost curve represents the various levels of outlay given by the prices of the two factors. The producer aims at producing the level of output at which his costs are least. He desires to minimize his cost for producing a given level of output. He will choose the combination of input, which minimizes his costs because only this can help him in earning maximum profit. The least cost combination of factors can be determined by comparing the production map in relation to a given cost line. The cost line is determined by the ratio of prices of two factors assuming a given investment fund with the firm and given prices of factors.

In the above figure the producer intends to produce 500 units of output with the combination of labour and machinery. The producer would be in equilibrium when he will produce the output at the minimum cost. This is achieved at point E when ON of machinery and OM of labour cost are incurred to produce the 500 units. The producer reaches this point when he is on the iso product

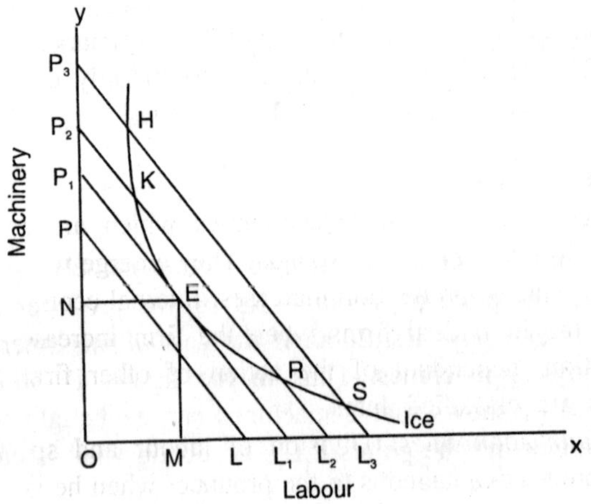

line P_1L_1, which is tangent to Iso quant curve. The other points HKRS lie above the tangent point of isoquant curve and indicate that the same level output is produced at a higher cost. Thus the producer will not choose any other combination apart from E. Point E is also on isocost line P_1L_1. It shows the ratio of the prices of labour and machinery being equal. Thus it can be said that a producer is in equilibrium when the marginal rate of technical substitution of two inputs is equal to the ratio of the prices of these inputs.

Marginal rate of technical substitution of labour for machinery is

$$\mathbf{MRT_{LM}} = \frac{\textbf{price of labour}}{\textbf{price of machinery}}$$

The equality between the rate of technical substitution between labour and capital to their price ratio gives maximum output at minimum cost.

5.6. ECONOMIES TO SCALE

The benefits obtained by business firms as a result of large scale production are referred to as economies to scale. Large scale production may be the result of large plant size, increase in the scale of production. Thus in a broad sense, anything which serves to minimize average cost of production in the long run as the scale of output increases is referred to as 'economies of scale'. Economies arise purely due to endogenous factors relating to efficiency of the entrepreneur or his managerial skills or the marketing strategy adopted. The economies to scale may be broadly classified into 1. Internal economies. 2. External economies.

Internal Economies

Internal economies are those economies which are open to an individual firm when its size expands. They emerge within the firm itself as its scale of production increases. Internal economies solely belong to the individual firms when the firm increases its scale of production, dependent of the action of other firms. Internal economies are classified into:

- ***Labour economies***: Division of labour and specialization becomes advantageous to the producer when he is producing on a large scale. Moreover a large firm attracts more efficient labour, as it can offer wide vertical mobility, prospects of promotion, as such the skill, efficiency and productivity of labour tend to grow leading to labour economies.

- ***Technical economies***: As a firm expands, it can use superior technique, capital goods, where as small firm cannot afford to install high quality machine. Increased use of machines leads to faster production, and better quality products. Production can be put to the optimum level. Bigger firms engage in experiment and research leading to better products. The expenditure on research may not have a bigger impact on the firm, but on the other hand a small firm cannot afford to make costly experiments. This can be because of the huge expenditure involved, and lack of qualified personnel to conduct the same.
- ***Economies of linked processes***: A large plant usually enjoys the advantage of linking processes. This is done by arranging production activities in a continuous sequence without any loss of time. For example, in the printing press the editing and printing of the news is taken out in the same place, this is in order to avoid wastage of time. Large units of machines and their continuous running by a large firm are often more economical in their power consumption as compared to a small machine. A large firm can avoid waste of its materials, which it can economically use for manufacturing certain by-products.
- ***Managerial Economies***: Large scale production gives the benefit of managerial specialization by creating departments entrusting to each a particular work such as purchase, stores, selling etc. Further considerable savings could be had in the general expenses. The overhead charges do not increase in proportion to increase in the size of business.

  A large firm will be in a better position to appoint a technical person who will be suitable and efficient in handling the production process. An entrepreneur can delegate his functions to trained and specialized personnel in his various departments.
- ***Marketing Economies***: A large firm can buy raw materials

at a cheaper cost since it would be buying a larger scale. Further a big firm also employs experts to purchase the required raw material more economically and in time. A large firm employs various marketing strategies and sell its products well, than the small firm.

- ***Financial economies***: Big farms are usually regarded less risky by investors, hence they may be willing to lend capital to such firms even at a lower rate of interest than to small firms. Big firms can easily raise their capital in the money market by issuing shares and debentures. The shares of a big concern number in lakhs but a small firm cannot hope to do so, because of its limited publicity.
- ***Risk bearing economies***: Since a large firm produces a large volume of output, it is in a position to bear the risks of losses and uncertainties. Since a large firm produces varied items, the loss in one of its products, can be compensated by the profit in the others. For instance in a restaurant, if the food items prepared are varied in nature, the demand would not exist for all the items at a time, if one of items are not demanded by the customers, the proprietor may face a loss, but if his size of operation is large the losses in one can be compensated by the other. In a large firm, there are less chances of disturbance as far as output of the product is concerned. The products on a large scale will have a wider market, thus the loss in one market can be compensated by the other.

External Economies

The benefits accruing to the industry as a whole because of its growth, the profit of which are shared by all the firms in the industry are called external economies. External economies are enjoyable by all the firms in the industry irrespective of their size.

Economies of localisation: When a number of firms are located in the same region, all of them tend to derive mutual benefits. Concentration of a particular industry in one area, in course of time, results in the development of conditions helpful to the industry. *For example*: training of skill labour. Labourers drawn from different restaurants can be given a training, the benefits of which can be obtained by all the restaurants who have sent their personnel for the training course.

Economies of information or market intelligence: When the firms expand their scale of operation, they indulge not only in increasing their production, but they also engage in research and development to further improve the product. The result of research is shared by all the firms in the industry, which improves their production and also profitability and also gain a better status over the other product competitors.

Economies of vertical integration: The growth of the industry will make it possible to split up production and the subsidiary jobs are efficiently done by specialized firms. *For example:* if the industry is engaged in ready made garments. The subsidiary work or the ancillary work like printing of the cloth or cutting of the cloth into different shapes and sizes is done only by those firms and the main job is done by the parent firm. This helps not only to increase production, but also saves time and provides employment to other firms.

Diseconomies to scale: When the expansion of the production process takes place beyond a certain level, it results in diseconomies to scale. This diseconomies can result in increasing the average cost of production, complexities in managing huge work force, labour problems, difficulties in coordination, increased risks, scarcity of factor supplies, financial difficulties. These act as delimiting factors in bringing down the production level and hinder the growth of the firm.

A brief analysis of the above chapter on production explains the activity of converting the raw material into a finished product. in the hotel industry also, this concept of conversion of input to output takes place in the form using various raw material to give the final product that is food. It thus becomes essential to understand the various concepts related the production function and its practical usuage in the production activity.

MODEL QUESTIONS

Short Questions

1. What is production function?

2. Explain the main difference between 'fixed costs' and variable cost.
3. What are isoquant curves?
4. Explain the difference between short run and long run in the production process.
5. What are internal economies?

Essay Questions

1. Explain the law of variable proportions.
2. What is meant by economies to scale? Explain with suitable example.

6
Cost of Production

6.1. MEANING

Production decisions are not possible without their respective cost considerations. Since resources are scarce and these have alternative uses, the use of these resources need sacrifice and hence cost. The firms will have to analyse these sacrifices whenever it decides to use the resources, and profits of the firm cannot be ascertained with analysing the cost involved in production.

Thus the cost analysis plays a key role in every business decisions. Though the hotel industry is a service sector, it works for profit, whether it provides hospitality in the form of providing food, accommodation or otherwise. Hence in providing these services it also has incur a certain amount of expenditure, which is simple words is termed as cost of production. The term 'cost of production' refers to the expenses incurred in the production of a commodity or when the raw material is converted into a finished product. For example, to provide an evening dinner to guests in a restaurant, various raw materials in the form of cereals, vegetables, fruits, and other items to prepare the final output that is the food, the various types of costs involved in producing this food item is known as the cost of production.

6.2. COST CONCEPTS RELATING TO PRODUCTION FUNCTION

Money cost: During the process of production, the producer uses various factors like land, labour, capital, raw material and organization to produce the final output. He does own the factor inputs, but has to obtain them for a price. For instance, he has to pay the rent, labourers their wages, capital borrowed the interest and so on. Thus the amount of money spent together on these factor inputs is known as the explicit cost or the money cost of production.

Opportunity cost: Opportunity cost is cost resulting from alternative opportunity that has been forsaken. It can be measured in terms of profits from the next best alternative venture that is forsaken by the firm by using the available resources. The main aim of production is not only the strain involved in producing a commodity, but the one which depends on the sacrifice of alternative product that could have been produced. Opportunity cost may also be defined as the 'cost of a given economic resource is the forgone benefits from the next best alternative use of that resource'.

The factors which are used in the manufacture of a product may also be used in the manufacture of other products. This means, factors of production are non-specific in nature and the producer can use them to suit his decisions. The opportunity cost of the production of a car can also used to manufacture a machine. For instance, if the farmer has a piece of agricultural land, he can use it to cultivate paddy or he can use to cultivate sugarcane also. The same land can also be used to construct a house, which he desires to rent out.

The concept of opportunity cost has great economic significance:

- The concept is based on the fundamental fact, that the means are scarce while the ends are unlimited, thus to utilize the means in an appropriate way, one commodity has to be produced at the cost of another.
- It is also used to explain the relative prices of different goods. For instance if the common input is used to produce two commodities, then the price of one output should be more or less appropriate to the price of another commodity. For example, on a piece of land 50 bags of paddy can be reaped, the same piece of land if used to produce sugarcane should be able to reap a crop which is equivalent to that of the value of 50 bags of paddy.
- The subject matter of economics speaks of scarcity or resources and alternative choices to be made. If the produc-

tion of one commodity is increased, then the resources have to be withdrawn, form production of other goods. Thus, when the resources are fully employed, then more of one good could be produced at the cost of producing less of the other.
- The concept of opportunity cost is essential for rational decision making by the producer. It serves as useful economic tool in analysing optimum resource allocation and rational decision making.

Explicit and Implicit cost

- Explicit costs are those expenses, which are actually paid by the firm. Also known as paid out cost, these costs appear in the accounting records of the firm. It is referred to the direct contractual monetary payments incurred through market transactions. They include—
  - Cost of raw materials
  - Wages and salaries
  - Power charges
  - Rent of the plant or building
  - Interest payment
  - Taxes like property taxes, licence, fee etc.
  - Miscellaneous involving marketing and advertising expenses.

Implicit cost also called book cost, refers to the opportunity costs of the use of factors, which a firm does not buy, or hire but which it already owns. Implicit costs are payments which are not directly or actually paid out by the firm. In fact they arise when the firm or entrepreneur supplies certain factors owned by himself. For instance the producer may use his own land for a restaurant rather renting one, for which rent is to be paid.

The explicit costs are important for the calculation of profit and loss account, but from the business point of view, the firm takes into account both the explicit and implicit cost.

Replacement cost and historical cost: Replacement cost refers to the price paid for the material currently prevalent in the market. Historical cost refers to original price incurred by the firm when it bought its raw materials. *Example*: if the price of a baking oven in 1998 was Rs. 3000, the present price for the same oven is

Rs. 4500, then the historical cost is Rs 3000 and the replacement cost is Rs. 4500.

Incremental and Sunk cost: Incremental costs refers to the additional cost incurred due to a change in the level or nature of production, for instance, adding a new product, a new machinery, etc. it measures the differences between old and new total costs. Sunk cost are costs which remain unaltered even after a change in the level or nature of business activity. For example paying interest on the entire investment is sunk cost.

Shut down cost and abandonment cost: Cost which would be incurred in the event of suspension of the plant operation and which would be saved if production continued is referred to as the shut down cost. Example, lay-off expenses, employment and training of workers, if the production is restarted. Abandonment cost refers to cost involved in disposing a plant, which may not required in the future. *Example*: ad-hoc manufacture of certain war equipments, whose production may not be needed in peace.

Accounting and Economic costs: Accounting cost are the actual or the outlay cost. These costs point to the expenditure already incurred. Accounting costs are helpful in managing taxation, to calculate profit or loss of the firm. Economic costs refer to the cost related to the future expenditure of the firm.

Selling cost: Refers to the expenditure incurred by the sellers in creating a demand for their product. Selling cost can include advertising expenditures, packaging, commission for marketing agents, traveling expenses for sales personnel. Margins granted to dealers in order to obtain their help them promote sales promotion, demonstration of goods and window display. It is also defined as selling costs incurred in order to enable the consumers be aware of the product availability and its utility.

Advertisement cost: Cost incurred by firms to market their products, to create effective demand is called advertisement cost. These are additional expenses, which the firms incur in order to obtain suitable market for the products and also to allow their products to become more competitive to that of the others.

Historical cost and replacement cost: Historical cost, also called the original cost refers to those costs which are originally incurred for production. This cost includes cost of plant, equipment, and material etc. where as replacement cost refers to the cost that firm would have to incur, if certain equipments (both an fixed and variable) are to be replaced. For example produce R incurred Rs. 10,000 to buy an equipment for his kitchen in 1997. The cost of the same equipment at the present market price is Rs. 18,000. Rs. 10,000 is the historical cost and Rs. 18,000 is the replacement cost.

SHORT RUN AND LONG RUN COST

The short run and long run cost depend on the time element involved in the production process. Short run cost are operating cost associated with the change in output, in the short period of time. In the short period only the variable factors can be changed and not fixed factors. Thus production involving only the variable cost in the short period is referred to the short run cost. It can also be stated as costs involved in partially changing the output.

Long run costs refers to the operating cost associated with the changing rate of output and changing the size of the plant. It also refers to those costs which are adaptable completely to the changes in the rate of output. These are costs, which can vary completely to a change in the production process.

The short run and the long run costs play an important role in business decisions, as it becomes important for the firm to take appropriate decisions in the short and long period. In the short period, only a few changes in the production process are possible, as the time involved is less. The cost involved here is also minimal. On the other hand in the long run period, the firm may decide to install a new plant, change the size of the existing one, or diversify in to a new product line. Thus the cost involved is quite large in the long run.

Fixed and variable factors: The inputs used in production involve both the fixed and variable inputs. Certain inputs like the plant, machinery, land can be utilized over a period of time. The investments on these inputs are expensive in nature. These inputs are called the fixed inputs or factors. Alternatively there are inputs like labour, raw material, which can be changed with in the short period of time. These are called the variable factors. Thus the costs incurred on variable factors are referred to as variable costs.

Fixed costs are those costs that are incurred as a result of the use of fixed factor inputs. They remain fixed at any level of output in the short run. The fixed cost remains constant in the short run period. They include payment of rent for building, or the purchase of the building, interest paid on capital, premium, depreciation and maintenance allowance, salaries, and property taxes. These costs are called the overhead cost.

Variable costs vary directly with the level of output. When the output is nil, they are reduced to zero. Variable costs are those that are incurred by the firm as a result of the use of variable inputs. Also called the prime cost or the direct cost, they represent all those costs which can be altered in the short run as the output changes. They include price of raw materials, wages on labour, fuel charges, excise duties, sales tax and charges on transport.

Full cost: Full cost refers to the average cost plus a flexible mark-up to cover the overhead costs and also to obtain a percentage of profit. In fixing prices, the firms like to cover not only their variable cost but also some amount of fixed costs. This practice of price fixation by the firms is called full cost pricing.

Social Cost: Social cost is the total cost of production, which includes the direct and indirect costs which the society has to pay for the output of the commodity. *Example*: slum clearance and town planning gives a face-lift to the locality, increasing the value of houses in them. Or, for instance in many industries, cost of research is borne by one producer, in bringing out an innovation, while other firms get free hint for improving their method of production. These cases are those in which the social cost incurred is lower than the private cost. Obtaining maximum social benefits is the goal of social costs.

Private cost: Private cost is the cost of producing a commodity by an individual producer. Here optimization of profit is the main goal behind incurring the private cost.

Total cost: Total cost is the aggregate expenditure by the firm in producing a given level of output. Total cost includes all kinds of cost, explicit as the implicit cost of production. It is also termed as a reward by the entrepreneur for his risk bearing capacity and also which allows him to stay in the business. As stated earlier there are some cost which can be varied with the increase in the output and there are certain costs which can be varied only in the long run period. Thus the total cost of a firm is the sum total of both the fixed and the variable cost.

In symbolic terms **Q = *f* {a,b,c, n},**

then TC = *f* (Q).

TC = TFC + TVC

Where, TC = total cost

TFC = total fixed cost

TVC = total variable cost.

Example: if the total fixed cost incurred to produce 50 shirts is Rs. 5000. The variable cost is Rs. 3000. Then the total cost is 5000 – 3000 = Rs. 8000.

Total fixed cost: The cost incurred by the firm on its fixed factors of production is referred to as the total fixed cost. The total fixed cost remains constant at all level of output.

TFC = TC – TVC

Example: To manufacture 20 pairs of shoes, total cost incurred is Rs. 3000 and Total variable Rs 1200 then the total fixed cost = 3000 - 1200 = Rs 1800.

Total variable cost: The cost incurred by the firm on the variable factors of production is referred to total variable cost. It is obtained by summing up the product of quantities of input multiplied by their prices.

TVC = TC – TFC

Or

TVC = *f* (Q),

which states that total variable cost is an increasing function of its output.

Example: To produce 50 Bags "A" needs a total cost of Rs. 300 and Total fixed cost of Rs. 200, the variable cost hence would be 300 – 200 = Rs. 100.

Average total cost: The per unit cost of production is called the average total cost. It is the total cost divided by the units of output. It is also the sum average of the average variable cost and average fixed cost.

$$ATC = \frac{TC}{Q}$$

Or

ATC = AVC + AFC

Average variable cost: It is the per unit variable cost of production. It is the total variable cost divided by the units produced.

$$AVC = \frac{TVC}{Q}$$

Average fixed cost: It is the per unit fixed cost of production. It also refers to the total fixed cost divided by the units produced.

$$AFC = \frac{TFC}{Q}$$

Marginal cost: It refers to the addition made to the total cost by producing one unit of the output. It may be defined as the cost of producing an extra unit of output. Marginal cost can also be defined as the change in the total cost with a change in the output. It can be calculated by dividing the change in total cost by one unit change in output. Symbolically it may written as:

$$MC_n = TC_n - TC_{n-1}$$

For example to produce 50 shirts a producer incurs a total cost of Rs. 1200. In order to produce 60 shirts he incurs a total cost of Rs. 1500.

The marginal cost here is: Rs. 1500 – Rs. 1200 = Rs. 300. It can also be written as

$$MC = \frac{\Delta TC}{\Delta Q}$$

Where Δ denotes change in output assumed to change by one unit. The marginal cost is independent of the size of the fixed cost in the short period.

Cost Schedule: The above concepts like the total fixed, the variable, average cost and the marginal cost, would help in deriving a imaginary demand schedule of a restaurant. Let us assume. The restaurant has an order to serve 800 guests. Now if we want to analyse the cost incurred per 100 individuals. The schedule goes as follows:

Output	TFC	TVC	TC	AC	AVC	AFC	MC
100	5000	-	5000	50	-	50	-
200	5000	2000	7000	35	10	25	2000
300	5000	3000	8000	26.6	10	16.6	1000
400	5000	3500	8500	21	8.8	12.5	500
500	5000	4200	9200	18.4	8.4	10	700
600	5000	5000	10000	16.6	8.3	8.3	800
700	5000	6000	11000	15.7	8.6	7.1	1000
800	5000	7500	12500	15.6	9.4	6.3	1500

Behaviour of the total cost curves

In the figure it is seen that **total fixed cost curve** takes the shape of straight line, which is parallel to the x-axis, which denotes the fixed nature of the fixed factor irrespective of the level of output. In the figure below, it is seen that the TFC curve from a point on the y axis. This shows that total fixed costs will be incurred even if the output is zero.

The **total variable cost curve** initially rises, becomes steeper, indicating a sharp increase in the variable cost with the increase in the level output. The upward rising total variable cost is related to the size to the output. It increases with the level of output, but the rate of increase is not constant. Initially, it increases at a

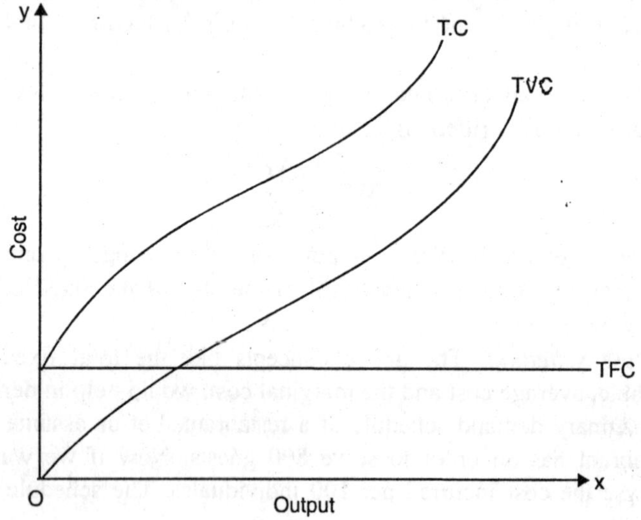

decreasing rate, but after a point, it increases at a diminishing rate. This is due to the operation of law of variable proportion, which indicates that the fixed cost being held constant in the short run, more of the variable cost have to be incurred to increase the level of output.

The TVC starts from the origin showing that when output is zero, the variable cost is nil. The TC curve lies above TVC curve. The total cost curve is the result of the variable and fixed cost. It is also seen that the TC and TVC curves have the same shape, since each increase in output increases total cost and variable cost.

The **total cost curve** is derived by vertically adding the total variable cost and fixed cost. The total cost is largely influenced by the variable cost in the short period. When the TVC curve becomes steeper, TC also becomes steeper, the vertical distance between TVC and TC curves represents the amount of total fixed cost.

6.3. BEHAVIOUR OF THE AVERAGE COST CURVES

Average fixed cost curve: It is the total fixed cost divided by the output. The average fixed cost decreases as the output increases, since the total fixed cost remains the same and is spread over more units, average fixed cost declines continuously. The AFC diminishes as the output increases. The AFC takes the shape of rectangular hyperbolar curve which moves from left to the right through its stretch. In mathematical terms the AFC curve approaches both the axis asymptotically. It gets very close to the x axis but never touches it.

Average variable cost curve: The average variable cost is the total variable cost divided by the number of units sold. The AVC curve is a 'U' shaped curve. The average variable cost curve decreases initially, reaches the minimum point and then rises. This is because as the output increases, the average variable cost decreases, it remains constant for a while and again starts to rise. This is due to the operation of the increasing, constant and diminishing returns.

Average cost curve: Since the average cost is the sum total of the average fixed and average variable cost. The Average cost curve becomes the vertical summation of the average fixed and

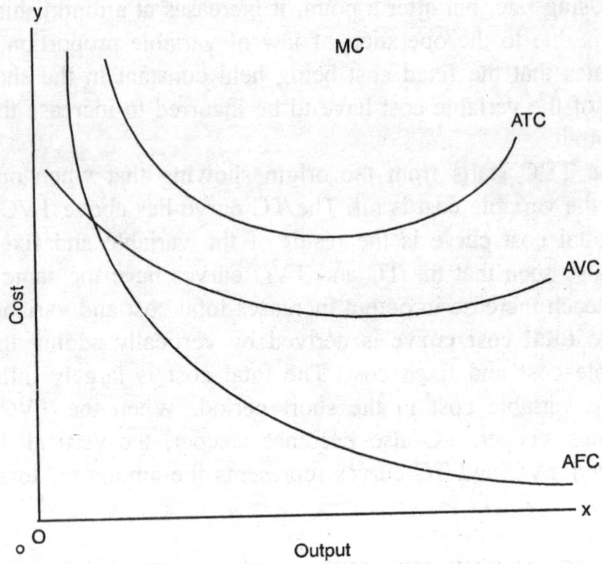

average variable cost. The AC curve also takes the 'U' shape, indicating that if the output is increased, the average cost decreases initially, than it remains constant for a while and then starts to increase. The average cost is also known as the unit cost since it is the cost per unit of output produced.

Marginal cost curve: The shape of the curve will be "U" one showing the marginal cost declining as the output expands, it remains constant for a while, and then starts to rise again. Marginal cost is the rate of change in total costs when output is increased by one unit. It is the slope of the total cost curve at the corresponding point. The slope of the MC curve also reflects of the diminishing returns is in operation. If increasing returns is in operation, the marginal cost curve will be declining as the cost will decrease with the increase in output. When the diminishing returns, is in operation, the MC curve will be ascending. The changes in the marginal cost is due to the changes in the variable cost irrespective of the changes in the output, as MC is independent of Fixed cost.

6.4. CHARACTERISTICS OF THE LONG RUN COST CURVE

Long run period denotes a period of time, wherein the firms can change their scale of operation with the help of both the variable and fixed factors of production. It is a period of time in which the firm can modify its product, diversify into a new product or even expand the existing one. The long run cost of production is the least possible cost of production of producing any given level of output, when all inputs become variable, including the size of the plant.

A set of short run periods becomes the long period. Hence it is also considered as the 'planning horizon', a period when the firm takes long term decisions with regard to the growth and the development of the product. Long run average cost is the long run total cost divided by the level of output. This curve depicts the least possible average cost of production at different levels of output.

DERIVATION OF THE LAC CURVE

The long run average cost curve is an envelope curve, which envelopes different short run average cost curves. In the figure below, the LAC curve is also derived and we would be finding the optimum level at which the firm can obtain the maximum output.

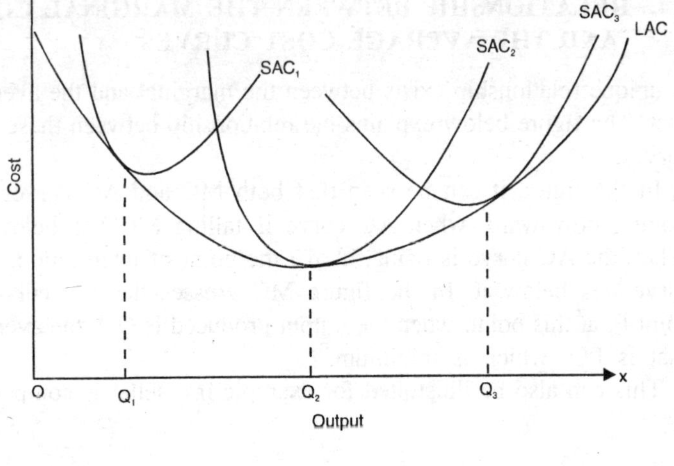

In the figure SAC_1, SAC_2 and SAC_3 are the short run average cost curves. These curves denote different plant sizes of the firm. In other words, it can be said that it represents different plant capacities. The LAC curve is drawn tangent to the three short run cost curves. It thus a flatter "U" shaped curve. The long run infact is nothing but the locus of all the tangent point of the short run curves. For instance, if the firm desires to produce a particular output in the long run, it will choose a position, which is the most ideal level and then build up a relevant plant. The producer when he is deciding on the level of output will decide on his course of action, in relation to the LAC curve. The optimum plant size is one at which the SAC is tangent to the LAC at its minimum point.

In the figure at OQ_2 level of out put, SAC is tangent to the LAC at both the minimum points. Thus, OQ_2 level of output, is regarded as optimum scale of output as it has the minimum points. The figure also indicates there is only one point where the LAC is tangent to the SAC at its minimum point. For instance though at OQ_3 level, the out put is more than the OQ_2 level. The cost incurred will be more. The LAC curve is less U-shaped curve. It gradually slopes downwards and after reaching a certain point it begins to slope upwards. This behaviour is attributed to the operation of the law of returns to scale. Increasing returns at the initial stage, decreasing, remaining constant for a while and again increasing. Thus LAC curve is also called the boat shaped curve.

6.4. RELATIONSHIP BETWEEN THE MARGINAL COST AND THE AVERAGE COST CURVES

A unique relationship exists between the marginal and the average cost. The figure below explains the relationship between these two curves.

In the figure it can be seen that both MC and AC curves are sloping downward, when AC curve if falling MC lies below it. When the AC curve is rising, above the point of intersection, MC curve lies below it. In the figure MC crosses the AC curve at point P, at this point, when the output produced is OQ, the average cost is PQ, which is minimum.

This can also be illustrated for example if a seller is comparing

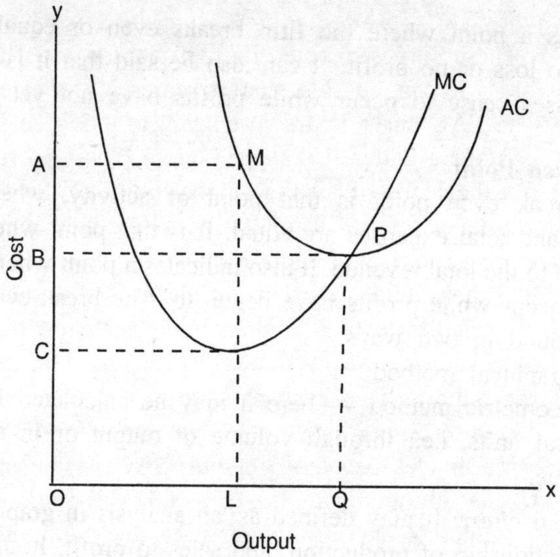

his average profit for a period of two months. In the first let us assume his average profit is 55 per cent. And in the second month if the average profit is less than the previous month i.e., less than 55 per cent, than average profit has fallen. On the other hand, if the average profit is more than 55 per cent, than it shows that his profit has increased. Thus marginal cost plays an important role in decision making, it has great significance, in determining equilibirium. Thus the short run curves, marginal cost, average variable and average fixed cost curve are all "U" shaped.

6.5. BREAK EVEN ANALYSIS

Since making profits is one of the main objective of the firms involved in the production process. Profit planning is therefore the utmost importance to the company. Break even analysis is one such technique utilized by the firms for proper profit planning of the firms.

It reveals the relationship between the volume and cost of production on the one hand, and the revenue and profits obtained from the sales on the other. The break even point is that level of sales where the net income is equal to zero. It indicates a zone which shows no profit or loss. In fact the word 'break even' symbolizes a point where the firm breaks even or equal where it faces no loss or no profit. It can also be said that it is a point where losses cease to occur while profits have not yet begun.

Break-Even Point

The break even point is that point of activity, where total revenues and total expenses are equal. It is that point where total cost equal to the total revenue. It also indicates a point where losses cease to occur while profits have begun to. The break-even point can be found in two ways.

1. The graphical method
2. The geometric method — here it may be calculated in terms of physical units, i.e., through volume of output or in terms of sales value.

Break-even chart: It may defined as 'an analysis in graphic form of the relationship of production, and sales to profit. It shows the extent of profit or loss to the firm at different levels of the activity. It depicts profit-output relationship. Thc break-even point can be explained through a schedule.

Break even schedule :

Output	Total Revenue	TFC	TVC	TC
0	0	500	-	500
100	500	500	400	900
200	1000	500	800	1300
300	1500	500	1200	1600
400	2000	500	1500	2000 BEP
500	2500	500	1600	2100
600	3000	500	1750	2250

In the table above, when the output is zero, total fixed cost is Rs. 500, and total cost Rs. 500, the total variable cost is nil. When the output is 100, the revenue is Rs. 500 and the total cost incurred is Rs. 900 which is more than the revenue. When the output is 200 units the revenue is Rs. 1000 and the cost still high at Rs. 1300. This trend continues till the firm produces 400 units of output. When the firm produces 400 units its total revenue is equal to the total cost. This is the break-even point of the firm, where

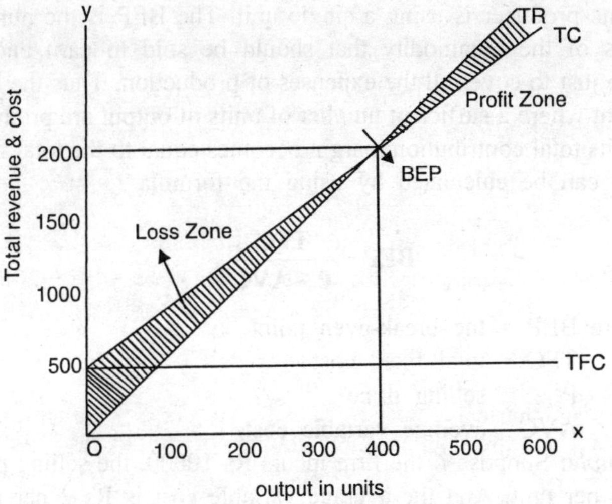

the total cost = total revenue. The firm if it produces beyond point, incurs less of cost, but obtains more of revenue.

The break even chart can also be illustrated through a figure. In the above figure, total cost and total revenue is measured on the Y axis, and output on the X axis. The TFC curve is a horizontal curve which is parallel to the X axis which indicates that total fixed cost remaining fixed with varying levels of output. The TR curve know total revenue curve lies above the total cost initially. The Total cost varies according to the variable cost, as a result of which it starts where the TFC curve ends. The break-even point occurs at 400 units. Where TR = TC, before the point of the break even it is seen that firm incurs losses because incurred is more than the revenue obtained at the break even point total revenue is equal to the total cost. Beyond this point it is seen that total revenue increases whereas the total cost falls.

Many economists consider the break-even as instrument for guiding the business in determining the profitable output. In the hotel industry the derivation plays an important role, as it acts as a seed money for reinvestment.

Geometric method

1. BEP in terms of physical units: This method can be used when the producer is using a single unit. The BEP is the number of units of the commodity that should be sold to earn enough revenue just to cover all the expenses of production. Thus the BEP is a point where a sufficient number of units of output are produced so that its total contribution margin becomes equal to the total fixed cost. It can be calculated by using the formula :

$$\mathbf{BEP} = \frac{\mathbf{TFC}}{\mathbf{P - AVC}}$$

Where BEP = the break-even point
TFC = total fixed cost
P = selling price
AVC= average variable cost.

Example: Suppose if the firm incurs Rs 10000, the selling price is Rs 4 per unit. And the average variable cost is Rs 2 per unit. Find the BEP?

$$\mathbf{BEP} = \frac{\mathbf{TFC}}{\mathbf{P - AVC}}$$

$= 10000 / 4 - 2$

$= 5000.$

Bep in terms of sales value: Bep in terms of physical output is suitable only in cost where single products are produced. If the firm is producing many products, the BEP can only be found in terms of sales value or in terms of total revenue. Here the contribution is a ratio to the sales.

$$\mathbf{BEP} = \frac{\textbf{Total Fixed Cost}}{\textbf{Contribution ratio}}$$

Contribution ratio is measured as:

$$\textbf{Contribution ratio (CR)} = \frac{\mathbf{TR - TVC}}{\mathbf{TR}}$$

Example: A firm incurs fixed cost of Rs 8000 and the variable cost is Rs. 12000. Its total sales receipt is Rs 30000 determine the Break even point.

$$CR = \frac{30000 - 120000}{30000}$$

$$= 3/5$$

$$BEP = TFC / CR$$

$$= \frac{3000 \times 5}{3}$$

$$= 13333$$

Assumptions of the Break even point

The break even analysis is based on certain assumptions. They include:

1. It assumes that costs can be classified into fixed and variable costs, thus ignoring semi-variable costs.
2. The selling price is assumed to be constant.
3. It assumes no change in technology, and labour efficiency.
4. It also assumes that production and sales almost remain fixed, in the sense there is no addition or subtraction to the inventory.
5. Factor prices are also assumed to remain constant.
6. The product mix is stable in the case of multi-product firm.

USES OF THE BREAK EVEN ANALYSIS

- It represents a microscopic picture of the business and it enables the management to find out the profitability region.
- It highlights the areas of economic strength and weakness of the firm.
- The BEA can be used to determine the 'safety margin'. The safety margin refers to a region where the firm can produce and sell without incurring loss. If the firm is working at loss, the safety margin helps in indicating a suitable increase in sales to reach the BEP and avoid losses. It can be found out by the following formula:

$$\textbf{Safety Margin} = \frac{\textbf{Sales} - \textbf{BEP}}{\textbf{Sales}} \times \textbf{100}$$

- *Target Profit*: The break even analysis will help in finding out the level of output and sales in order to reach the target of profit fixed.

$$\textbf{Target sales volume} = \frac{\textbf{Fixed cost} - \textbf{target profit}}{\textbf{Conbtribution margin \%}}$$

(Contribution margin = selling price – variable cost).

- *Change in price*: Many factors have to be considered before reducing the price of a product. Reduction in price need not necessarily result in increased sales, as it depends on the elasticity of demand.

$$\textbf{New sales volume} = \frac{\textbf{Total fixed cost} + \textbf{total profit}}{\textbf{New selling price} - \textbf{Average variable cost}}$$

Thus the break even analysis serves as an important tool in helping entrepreneurs to take appropriate decisions, as far as pricing policy, sales projection and revenue of the firm is concerned.

The study on cost and cost concepts helps the entrepreneur in the hotel industry. Since this industry also strives to work for profit. An understanding of various cost concepts is needed not only to know the various type of expenditure involved in production process, but also helps to produce at the optimum level with the minimum cost. The relationship between revenue and cost which is well explained through the break even analysis, helps the industry to operate within the safe region of profit making, it helps to determine the level of output at which the industry can make profits or losses.

MODEL QUESTIONS

Short Questions

1. Explain the term cost of production.
2. What is opportunity cost?
3. How is the marginal cost calculated?
4. What are selling costs?
5. Explain the relationship between cost, volume and output in the hotel industry.
6. Differenciate between fixed and variable cost.
7. What is social cost?
8. What is explicit cost?
9. When the advertisement cost appear in business?

Essay Questions

1. Give an imaginary cost schedule.
2. Why is the average revenue curve 'U' shaped? Explain.
3. How is the long run average revenue curve derived?
4. How is the break even analysis useful in business decisions?

7
Supply

7.1. MEANING

One of the market forces, which affect the price of a commodity is Supply. Supply acts just the opposite of demand in that, it is directly proportional to the changes in price. Supply in ordinary language means the stock of goods at a given point of time in the market. It may also be the amount of goods offered for sale at a price. The supply of a commodity may be defined as the amount of that commodity which the sellers are able and willing to offer for sale at a particular price during a certain period of time.

Prof Mc Connel defines supply, "as a schedule which shows the various amounts of a product which a producer is willing to and able to produce and make available for sale in the market at each specific price in a set of possible prices during some given period". Thus supply always means supply at a given price.

7.2. SUPPLY AND STOCK

- Supply is the outcome of stock, that is the amount of the commodity produced which is offered for sale in the market.
- Stock determines the supply of a commodity, the stock in hand is the actual quantity that is offered in the market. For example a producer has 1000 units of a commodity, but he sells only 700 units of the commodity. 700 units become the actual supply.
- It is said that stock is the outcome of production, what is produced becomes the potential stock and supplied to the market for sale. Increase in actual supply can exceed the

increase in current stock, when along with the fresh stock, old accumulated stock is also released for sale at the prevailing price.

7.3. THE LAW OF SUPPLY

The law of supply states that other factors remaining constant, when the price of a commodity increases, supply increases and when the price of a commodity decreases supply decreases. It can be defined as 'others things being constant, the price of a commodity has a direct influence on the quantity supplied, as the price of a commodity rises, its supply is extended; as the price falls, its supply is çontracted'. Large quantities are supplied at higher prices and small quantities are supplied at lower prices.

Explanation of the law

The law of supply can be explained through a schedule. The supply schedule explains the quantities of commodities that can be supplied at varying prices.

Supply Schedule

Price of apples(per kg)	*Amount supplied (per week)*
15	50
20	70
30	100
45	200

From the above schedule, we understand that when the price is the highest i.e., Rs. 45 the quantity supplied is also highest i.e., 200 kgs., but on the other hand when the price falls the quantity supplied falls. It is thus seen that when the price is Rs 15, the quantity supplied is 50 kgs. It can therefore be seen that the supply of commodity increases when the price increases and vice versa.

The law of supply can also be explained through a figure. In the figure below, price is measured on the y axis and quantity supplied on the x axis. The supply curve SS, slopes from the left to the right upwards. When OP is the price, OQ is the quantity demanded, when the price increases to OP_1, the quantity supplied increases to OQ_1. Alternatively if the price falls to OP_2, the quantity supplied decreases to OQ_2. Thus the law of supply indicates a direct relationship between price and the quantity supplied.

Assumptions underlying the law of supply

Cost of Production: The cost of production is assumed to remain unchanged. If it increases along with the rise in the price of the product, the sellers will not find it worthwhile to produce more. It also implies that factors prices like wages, interest, rent, are also unchanged.

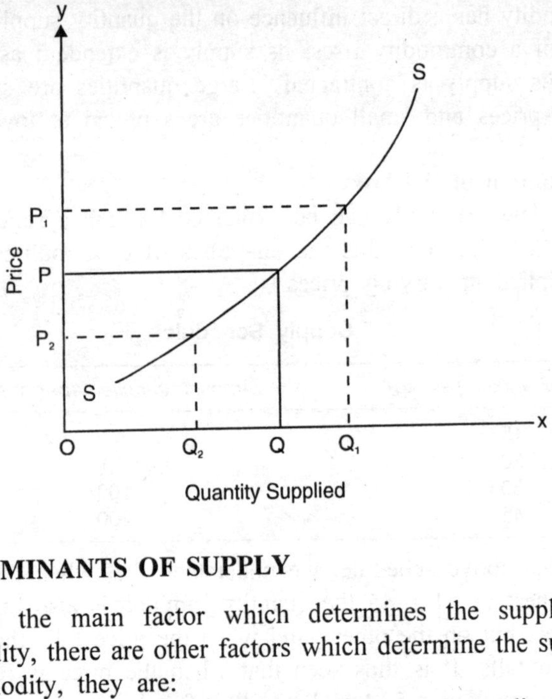

DETERMINANTS OF SUPPLY

Price is the main factor which determines the supply of a commodity, there are other factors which determine the supply of a commodity, they are:

- ***State of Technology***: Supply of a commodity largely depends on its production, which inturn depends on technology in use. If the technology is an outdated, it leads to a decrease in output which affects supply. Advancement in science and technology act as powerful forces influencing productivity.
- ***Sellers***: The supply of the commodity also depends on the

number of firms or sellers in the market. When the sellers are few, the supply will be small. If they are large in number, the supply will also be large.

- *Cost of production*: If the cost involved in producing the product is high, it leads to a decrease in supply, if the cost of production is less owing to other factors, increases production, this inturn leads to an increase in supply.
- *Prices of related factors*: Though the supply of a commodity depends on its price, at times it can change due to the price of related factors. For instance in case of substitutes, if the price of a substitute commodity falls, it affects the supply of the other substitute commodity already in use.
- *Natural factors*: The supply of commodities also gets affected due to other natural factors which are outside the economic sphere. For example when maharastra got affected by the earth quake, the exports of textile from that state got affected. If there is drought in Andhra pradesh, the supply of rice from that place gets affected.
- *Tax and subsidy*: A tax on the commodity increases its cost of production and thereby supply, where as a subsidy acts as an incentive to increase production and supply.

7.4. SUPPLY FUNCTION

In algebraic terms, the supply function can be written as:

$$\mathbf{S_x = f\{P_X, P_F, P_Y, \ldots\ldots P_Z, O, T, t, s\}}$$

Where S_x = the supply of commodity x.

P_x = price of x.

P_t = prices of factor inputs employed to produce commodity x.

P_y .....Pz = the prices of goods.

O = factors outside the economic sphere

T = technology used

t = commodity taxation

s = subsidy

Assumptions underlying the law of supply

- *Cost of Production*: It is assumed that the cost of producing the product remains unchanged. If there is increase or decrease in the cost of production, the normal flow of supply gets affected. Therefore, the law of supply is valid only if the cost of production remains constant. The factor prices like wages, rent, interest, prices of raw materials are assumed to be fixed.

- ***Technology***: The method of production also remains constant. If the technology, improves, leading to increase in production levels. The supplier would be supplying more even at falling prices.
- ***Government Policies***: Policies of the government like the taxation, trade policy should be constant. If there is an increase or a fresh levy of excise duties or if certain quotas are fixed for the components used in production, then more supply would not be possible even at higher prices.
- ***Transport costs***: The transport cost of carrying the finished goods is assumed to remain fixed.
- ***Speculation***: If the sellers speculate the future changes in the prices of the product. For instance, if they anticipate a fall in the price of the commodity, they would intent to supply more even at falling prices, instead allowing the commodities to perish.
- ***Prices of substitute commodities***: The law assumes that there are changes in the prices of other products. If the price of other product rises faster than that of the given product, producers might transfer their resources to the other product, which is more profit yielding, due to rise in prices.

7.5. ANALYSIS OF SUPPLY

Though the price of a commodity plays a major role in determining the supply. There can various factors which also play a role in determining the supply. The analysis tries to how the price and various factors affect the supply of the commodity. The analysis can be made through the: 1.Extension and contraction of Supply 2. Increase and decrease of Supply.

1. Extension and contraction of Supply

Other things remaining same, when supply increases due to an increase in price. It is known as extension of supply. When the

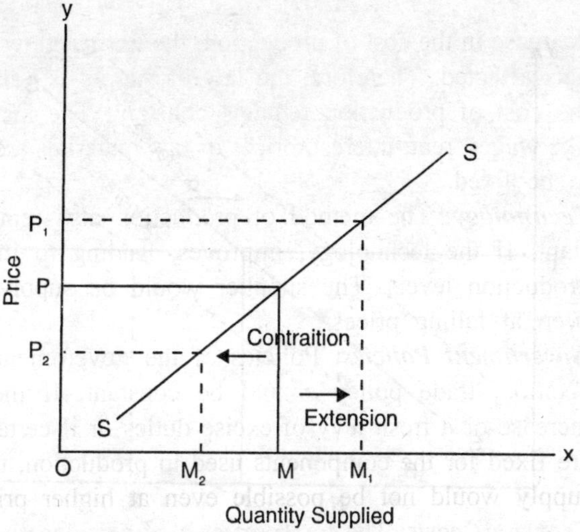

supply falls due to a fall in price, it is known as contraction of supply. This can be explained through a figure.

In the figure, SS is the supply curve, at OP price, OM is the quantity supplied. When the increases to OP_1, the quantity supplied increases to OM_1. This movement of the from OM to OM_1 is referred to as the extension of supply. Alternatively if the price falls from OP to OP_2, the quantity supplied falls from OM to OM_2. This Movement from OM to OM_2 is known as contraction of supply.

2. Increase and Decrease of Supply

The supply of a commodity also changes due to a change in other determinants like weather conditions, prices of factor inputs, technology. When the supply increases, price being constant, it is known as increase of supply, the price being constant, when the supply decreases it is known as decrease in supply.

The above figure explains the increase and decrease in supply. In the figure it is seen that the price remains constant at OP. The price being constant, the supply moves to upwards to its new Position S_1S_1,the quantity supplied changes from ON to ON_1. This movement of the supply curve from ON to ON_1 is known as the decrease in supply. On the other hand the price remaining constant,

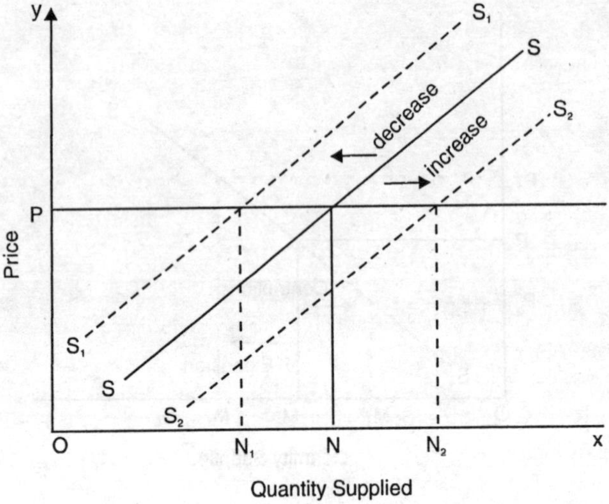

if the supply curve SS moves from downwards to S_2S_2, this movement from ON to ON_2 is known as the increase in supply.

7.6. ELASTICITY OF SUPPLY

Elasticity of supply measures the rate of change in supply due to a change in price. The word 'change' implies both 'increase' and 'decrease' in the supply of the commodity. It can also stated that it indicates the proportionate change in the quantity supplied due to proportionate change in the price.

The elasticity of supply can be algebraically stated as

$$E_s = \frac{\textbf{Proportionate change in quantity supplied}}{\textbf{Proportionate change in price}}$$

In symbolic terms it may written as

$$E_s = \frac{\Delta q_s}{\Delta p} \times \frac{p}{q_s}$$

Where Δq_s = change in quantity supplied

Δp = change in price

p = initial price

q_s = initial quantity supplied

Example: Suppose the price of a commodity is Rs. 500, 400 units of it is supplied. For example if the price rises to 800, the quantity supplied also increases to 500 units. The elasticity of supply is $E_s = \frac{500}{2500} \times \frac{200}{100}$

$E_s = 4$

The elasticity of supply may be broadly classified into two categories depending upon its intensity:

Elastic Supply: When the proportionate change in the quantity supplied is greater than the proportionate change in price, it is known as elastic supply.

Inelastic Supply: When the proportionate change in the quantity supplied is less than the proportionate change in price, it is known as inelastic supply.

The elasticity of supply can also be classified in to five different categories:

1. relatively elastic supply
2. relatively inelastic supply
3. perfectly elastic supply
4. perfectly inelastic supply
5. unitary elastic supply

1. Relatively elastic supply:

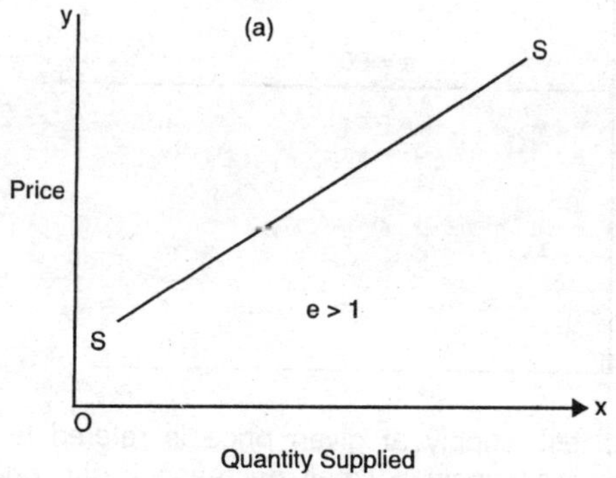

In the figure the Supply cure Ss is a flatter curve indicating that a slight change (i.e., increase or decrease) can being about a great change in supply. The value of elasticity here is e > 1.

2. Relatively inelastic supply:

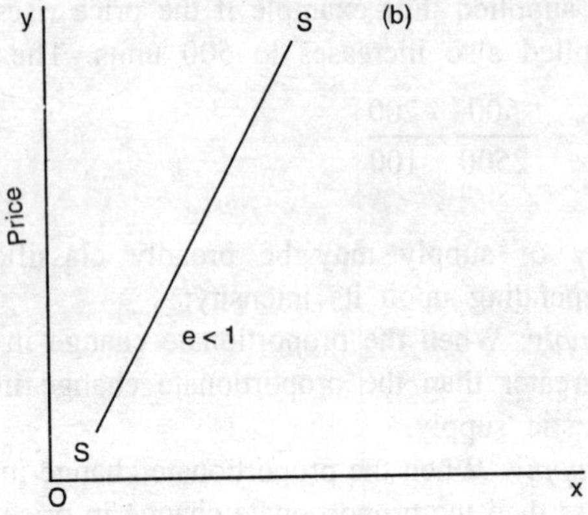

The Supply curve has a very steep position. This is because when the supply is inelastic a greater change in price will bring a less then proportionate change in supply. The value of elasticity here is e < 1.

3. Perfectly elastic supply:

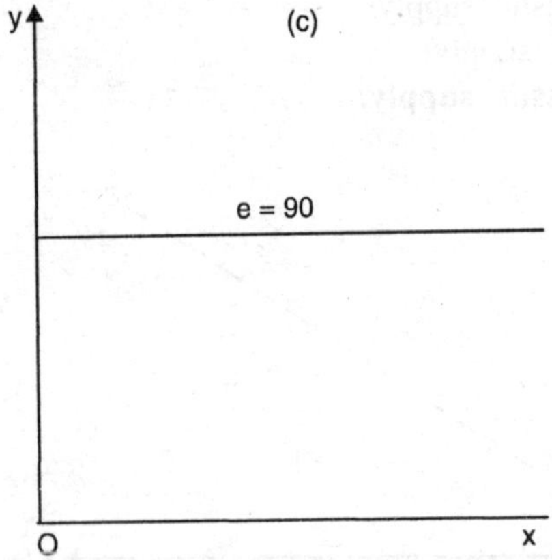

An end less supply at given price is refered to as perfectly elastic supply a small decrease is the price will fully stop the supply an unelastic situation the value of elasticity here is $e = \infty$

4. Perfectly inelastic supply:

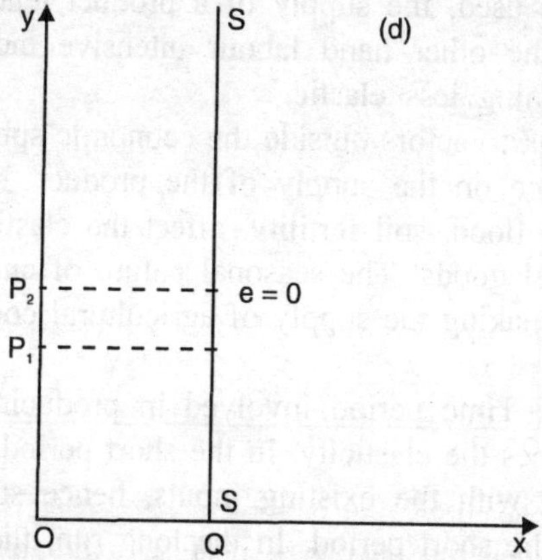

Supply is perfectly inelastic when the supply does not show any change either to an increase or decrease in price the supply remains constant. This can occur when the market supply exists just for a day in case of supply of vegetables and fruits. The value of elasticity is e = 0.

5. Unitary elastic supply:

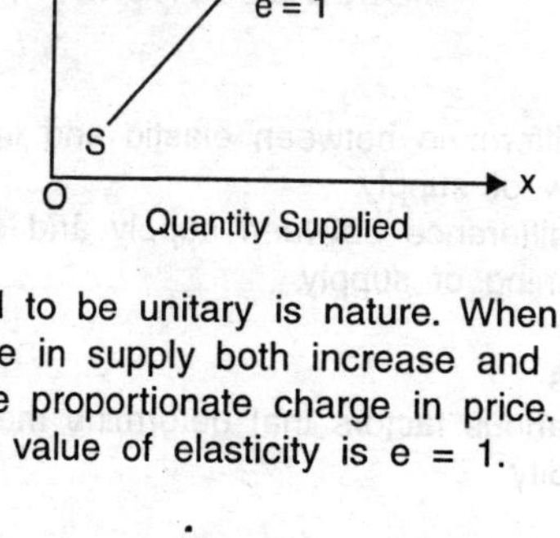

Supply is said to be unitary is nature. When the proportionate change in supply both increase and decrease is equal to the proportionate charge in price. Here the value of elasticity is e = 1.

Factors determining elasticity of supply

- *Technique of production:* When capital intensive method of production is used, the supply of a product tends to be more elastic. On the other hand labour intensive method leads to supply becoming less elastic.
- *Natural factors*: Factors outside the economic sphere also wield great influence on the supply of the product. Natural factors like weather, flood, soil fertility, affect the elasticity of supply of agricultural goods. The seasonal nature of cultivation is the main factor making the supply of agricultural commodities less elastic.
- *Time period*: Time period involved in producing the product also determines the elasticity. In the short period, the stock can be increased with the existing inputs, hence supply becomes inelastic in the short period. In the long run, the stock can be adjusted to a greater extent by producing with a changing scale of production, by the changing the size of plant, production capacity. Thus in the long period, supply tends to be relatively elastic.
- *Availability of markets*: If the producers find less markets for their produce, the supply is said to be inelastic in nature. On the other hand if the producers find suitable markets, then the supply tends to become elastic in nature.
- *Scale of production*: Goods produced on a large scale have inelastic supply for their products. While goods produced on a small scale have a relatively inelastic supply.

MODEL QUESTIONS

Short Questions

1. Explain the difference between elastic and inelastic supply.
2. Define the law of supply.
3. What is the difference between supply and stock?
4. Give the meaning of supply.

Essay Questions

1. Explain the various factors that determine the elasticity of supply for a commodity.

8
Revenue Analysis

The commodities, which are produced by the producer are offered for sale at a particular price with a certain percentage of profit added to it. Thus the amount of money, which the producer gets out of the sale of his products, is referred to as Revenue.

Revenue also means sale receipts. Revenue is nothing but the price multiplied by the number of units of commodity offered for sale. The total amount of money received by the producer when he offers his commodities for sale is known as total revenue.

8.1. TOTAL REVENUE

Total revenue is the total sale receipts of the output produced over a given period of time, total revenue depends on two factors, i.e., the price of the product and quantity of the product. In symbolic terms: **Total revenue = price × quantity sold.**

For example, when a producer sells 50 units of the product, the price of each being 15 per unit. The total revenue is 50 × 15 = 750

8.2. AVERAGE REVENUE

Average revenue is total revenue divided by the number of units sold. Revenue obtained per unit of output sold is also termed average revenue.

$$\mathbf{AR} = \frac{\mathbf{TR}}{\mathbf{Q}}$$

Where AR = Average revenue
TR = Total revenue
Q = Quantity of the commodity sold.

For instance if TR is Rs. 10000 and units sold is 200 units.

Average revenue = Rs. 10000/200

= Rs. 50

By definition average revenue is the price. Price of a commodity is always per unit. Thus sales per units is also called average revenue.

AR = TR / Q, since TR = P × Q

As AR = P × Q / Q

Thus AR = P

8.3. MARGINAL REVENUE

Marginal revenue is the change in total revenue resulting from an increase in sale by an additional unit of the product at a point of time. It can also be said that the addition made to the total revenue by selling one more unit of the commodity.

It can also be expressed that the marginal revenue is the addition made to the total revenue by selling 'n' units of a product instead of 'n – 1', where 'n' is any given number, per period of time.

$$MR_n = TR_n - TR_{n-1}$$

Where MR_n = marginal revenue of the out put sold.

TR_n = Total revenue of the out put sold.

TR_{n-1} = Total revenue earned by selling n – 1 units per period of time.

Example: The producer is selling 200 units of the commodity and his total revenue is Rs. 2000. If he were to sell 205 units of commodity. His total revenue would Rs. 2100. Hence his marginal revenue is Rs. 2000 – Rs. 2100 = Rs. 100.

Thus marginal revenue is also defined as the ratio of change in total revenue to a unit change in output sold.

It can also written as $\mathbf{MR} = \dfrac{\mathbf{dTR}}{\mathbf{dQ}}$

The concept of marginal revenue is of great significance to the producer, as it helps him to find the additional profit obtained at a point of time. It denotes the rate of change in total revenue as the sale of output change per unit.

8.4. RELATIONSHIP BETWEEN PRICE AND REVENUE UNDER PERFECT COMPETITION

In perfect competition, the firm cannot influence the market price, infact the firm is a price taker. Hence the total revenue of the firm increases proportionately with the output. When the total revenue increases in direct proportion, the average revenue also remains constant, this is because the price is not affected by the output and what ever is produced has to be sold at the market price. Since the market price is constant without any variation, the marginal revenue and the average revenue will be equal and constant. In such cases the marginal revenue will be a parallel straight line to the x axis.

No. of Units sold	*Average revenue AR = price*	*Total revenue*	*Marginal revenue*
1	5	5	5
2	5	10	5
3	5	15	5
4	5	20	5
5	5	25	5
6	5	30	5

In the above column 2 shows that price and AR are equal and constant. The total revenue proportionately varies with the output. Thus the marginal revenue becomes equal to the average revenue and price.

Diagrammatic representation

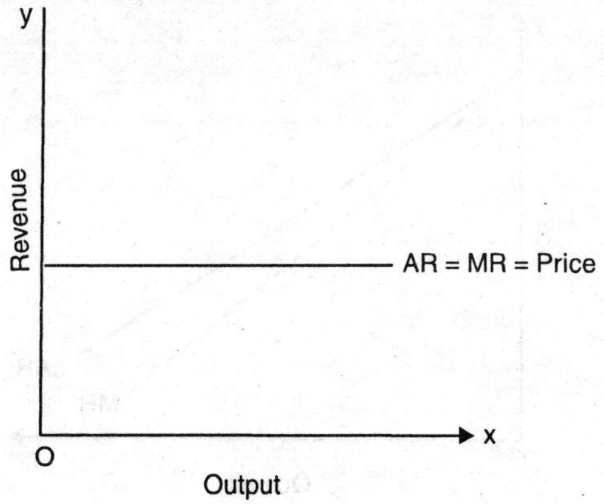

In the above figure revenue is measured on the y axis and output on the x axis. In case of the firm operating under conditions of perfect competition, its average, marginal revenue for one identical curve which is parallel to the x axis. The TR curve moves upward to the right, but its slope is constantly positive at 45° level indicating that revenue increases in direct proportion to the output.

Under Imperfect Competition

Under imperfect competition, whether it is monopoly, monopolistic competition or oligopoly, the average revenue curve slope downwards. It is also the demand curve of the firm. Under imperfect competition, a firm can sell larger quantities only when it reduces the price. When the output is increased, the price has to be reduced. Hence the average curve is a declining curve, and likewise the marginal revenue also slope downwards.

No of units sold	Price AR	TR	MR
1	10	10	10
2	9	18	8
3	8	24	6
4	7	28	4
5	6	30	2
6	5	30	0

The schedule explains the movement of the average revenue, as the units keep increasing the price of the commodity gradually decreases, the total revenue increases, but at a diminishing rate. The marginal revenue also decreases and gradually reaches a zero level.

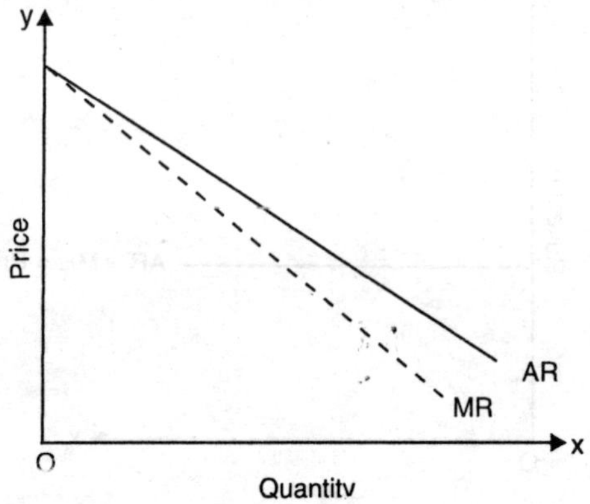

The figure above illustrates the movement of the AR and TR curves. The curves show that AR and MR are declining. The MR curve lies below the AR curve. Since the value of the marginal revenue diminishes faster than the average revenue, it is seen that the marginal curve slopes downwards and falls below the average revenue curve.

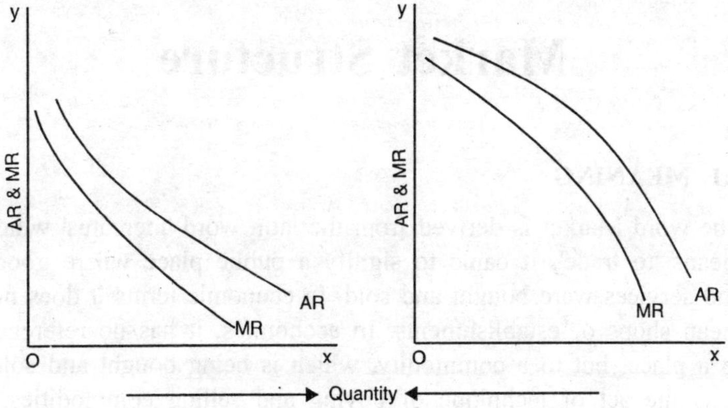

The average revenue and the marginal revenue curves need not be a straight line. They may either be convex or concave. But in all cases, the MR curve lies below the AR curve.

The revenue analysis helps in understanding how the revenue is calculated. It also states how the firms should produce the commodity and fix its price under the varied competitive situation. In relating these concepts to the hotel industry, revenue analysis states how the industry while offering its various services — be it providing food, accommodation and others should react under different competitive situations.

MODEL QUESTIONS

Short Questions

1. Explain the concept of revenue.
2. How is the average revenue calculated?
3. Find the difference between the total revenue and marginal revenue.
4. Explain the behaviour of the average revenue under imperfect competition.

9

Market Structure

9.1. MEANING

The word Market is derived from the latin word 'mercatus' which means 'to trade'. It came to signify a public place where goods and services were bought and sold. In economic terms it does not mean shops or establishments. In economics, it has no reference to a place, but to a commodity, which is being bought and sold. It is the act or technique of buying and selling commodities.

According to Benham "market is any area which buyers and sellers are in close touch with one another, either directly or through a dealer, that the price obtainable in one part of the market affects the prices paid in other parts". Stonier and Hague explain market as "any organization whereby buyers and sellers of a good are kept in close touch with each other… there is no need for a market to be in a single building… the only essential for a market is that all buyers and sellers should be in constant touch with each other, either because they are in the same building or because they are able to talk to each other by telephone at a moment's notice". Thus market refers to a place where buyers and sellers meet for the common purpose of exchanging commodities for money.

Thus the market has four important components:

- ***Commodity:*** Each commodity has a separate market. In the sense that every commodity has a separate set of buyers and sellers. Thus market in this way is considered to be a place where buyers and sellers with a common interest meet.
- ***Price:*** The exchange of commodities between the buyers and sellers occurs at a particular price, which is mutually agreeable to both the buyers and sellers of the commodity.

- ***Sellers:*** Unless a commodity is offered for sale in the market, there is no question of any one buying the commodity. Therefore, for any market, the existence of sellers is another necessity.
- ***Consumers:*** There should be demand from the consumers side. In a place where people are poor, there would very less demand or no demand for the commodities.

9.2. CLASSIFICATION OF MARKETS

Markets are basically divided based on the area, nature of transactions, volume of business, time, sellers, regulation and nature of the competitive situation.

1. Area: Markets where transactions takes place in the locality, village or city, they are called local markets. In the local markets transactions take place for perishable goods. In the regional and national markets, the regional and national conditions play a role in these markets. International market consists of transactions between the nationals of different countries. It takes place in durable consumer goods, producer goods and precious metals.

2. Nature of transactions: Here markets are classified into spot market and future market. When goods are exchanged on the spot it is as the spot market. Transactions involving agreements of future exchange of goods are referred to future markets.

3. Volume of business: Depending on the quantity of goods offered by the sellers markets can be classified in to the wholesale markets and the retail markets. Whole markets are markets where commodities are sold on a wholesale basis, the prices in these markets are much cheaper compared to the prices in the retail market. Retail market is a place where commodities are sold on a retail basis. Here the volume of transaction is limited and is less compared to the wholesale market.

4. Sellers: Markets are also divided on the status of the sellers- the primary market, the secondary market and the terminal market. The primary market is one where the manufacturers produce and supply to the wholesalers. In the secondary market the wholesalers act as intermediaries between the manufacturers and retailers. The retailers who sell the commodities to the final consumers constitute the terminal market.

5. Nature of competition: Depending on the competitive situation prevailing, the markets are classified into the perfect competitive market, where the competition exists but on perfect terms. In a imperfect competitive situation, the competition is very intense between the sellers where they resort to price wars, under cutting of prices in order to capture the market.

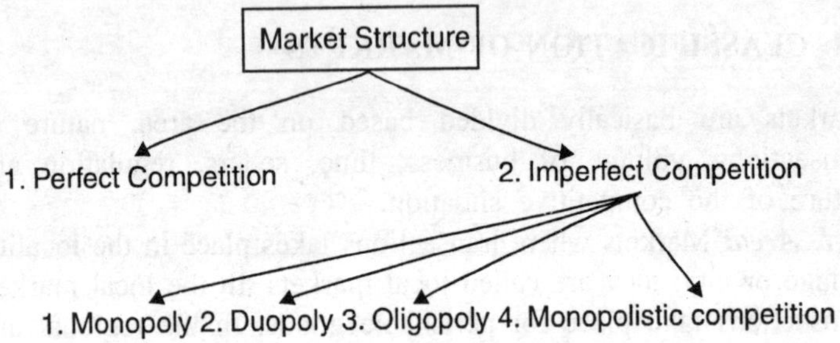

The market structure is basically divided depending on the competitive situation prevailing in the market. It is thus into :

1. The perfect competitive situation
2. Imperfect competitive situation.

9.3. PERFECT COMPETITION

Perfect competition is a market situation which is characterized by group of sellers who sell a similar product at a homogeneous price. In this type of market a single market price prevails for the commodity which is determined by the forces of total demand and total supply in the market. Every seller sells his/her commodity at the prevailing price. Thus in a perfect market, the producer is known as the price taker. Mrs Joan Robinson defines perfect competition in terms of elasticity of demand. According to her, "In perfect competition there will be perfect elasticity of demand for the product of every individual producer. There should be large number of sellers, and the buyers should be aware of the various price offers and their perfect conditions, so that they have no reason to prefer one seller to another".

Characteristic feature of a perfect market

There are certain distinct feature which characterize the perfect market:

1. Large number of sellers: A perfect market is characterized by a large group of sellers who sell similar products at a uniform price. Since the market comprises a large number of sellers, each firm's size is only a percentage of the market supply. Consequently any variation in individual supply has a very little effect on the total supply. Thus, an individual firm cannot exert any influence on the ruling market price. This is the main reason behind referring to the sellers in this market as a 'price taker'.

2. Large number of buyers: There are a large number of potential buyers in a perfectly competitive market. Since the number is large, each buyers demand constitutes just a fraction of the total market demand. Hence no individual buyer is in a position to exert his influence on the prevailing price of the product.

3. Product Homogeneity: Sellers sell homogeneous product. In other words, the product of each seller is virtually standardized. Since, each firm produces an identical product. Their products, can be readily, substituted for each other. The buyer has no specific preference to buy from a particular seller only. Thus his purchase is only a matter of chance and not of choice, on account of the homogeneity of goods.

4. Free entry and exit of firms: There is free entry of new firms into the market. There is no legal, technological, economic, financial or any other barrier to their entry and exit. Thus the mobility of firms ensures that whenever there is scope in the business new entry will take place ad competition will remain always stiff. Due to the stiff competitive situation inefficient firms naturally quit from the market.

5. Perfect knowledge of the market conditions: the buyers and sellers must have a perfect knowledge of the prevailing market conditions, especially the prevailing price, quantities and source of supply and quality of the product. In order to prevent discrepancies in the prices of commodities, the consumers should also be aware of the prevailing price.

6. Non-intervention of the government: Perfect competition also implies that there is no government intervention in the working of the market economy. There are no tariffs, subsidies, rationing of the goods, control of supply of the raw material, licensing, or other government interference. The non-intervention is necessary in order to enable the forces of demand and supply to work freely.

7. ***Absence of transport cost:*** Since all the firms are located in a particular geographical area, the transport cost is equally borne out by all the firms in the market. Hence the percentage of cost incurred is equally shared by all the firms.

Price determination under Perfect Competition

Price under perfect competition is determined by the interaction of demand and supply. Though individual buyers and sellers cannot influence the price of the commodity, the aggregate demand and supply play a great role in influencing the price of the commodity. The demand curve normally is a convex curve sloping from the left to the right downwards indicating that the consumers would buy more commodities at less prices and less commodities at high prices. The supply curve on the other hand, slopes from left to right upwards, indicating the suppliers would supply more at high prices and supplying less at low prices. The level at which the demand curve intersects the supply curve determines the equilibirium price. Equilibirium price is that price at which quantity demanded is equal to the quantity of the product supplied. At this price the two forces, demand and supply, balance each other and balanced quantity is called the equilibirium quantity.

Market demand and supply schedule for wheat

Price Per kg	*Total Demand per week*	*Total supply per week*	*pressure on price*
6.0	2000	10000	downward
5.0	3000	8000	downward
4.5	4000	6000	downward
3.0	5000	5000	neutral
2.0	6000	4000	upward
1.5	7000	2000	upward

The equilibirium price can be explained through the above schedule. In the table when the price of wheat is Rs. 6, the total demand of wheat for a week is 2000 kg, but the supply is 10000 kg, 8000 kg remain unsold, hence there is downward pressure on price. Similarly when the price is Rs. 5 the demand is 3000 kg and total supply is 8000 kg. There is again a down ward pressure on price due to the surplus supply. This continues to occur till the price reaches Rs. 3. When the price of wheat is Rs. 3 per kg, the total demand is 5000 kg and total supply is 5000 kg. It is seen here that the total supply is equal to the total demand for the commodity, the equilibirium price is thus determined at Rs. 3 when the supply is equal to the demand. If there is further increase in demand for wheat due to a fall in price the supply falls short of demand. For instance, if the price is Rs. 2, the total demand is 6000 kg and supply is only 4000 kg. Hence the surplus demand forces the price increase, thus there is upward pressure of price. This continues till the equilibirium price is reached.

The derivation of equilibirium price under perfect competition can also be explained through a figure.

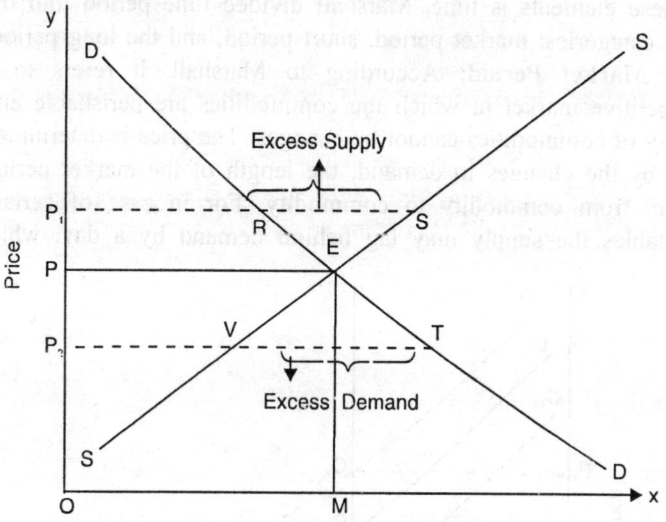

In the figure DD is the demand curve which slopes downward from the left to the right downwards. SS is the supply curve which slopes upwards from left to the right. The price is measured on the y axis and quantity supplied and demanded is measured on the x axis. The demand and supply curve intersect at E, the equilibirium point. The corresponding price OP at which the quantity supplied and demanded is OM. Suppose the price increases above the equilibirium price. At OP_1 the demanded is only P_1R while the supply is P_1S. The excess supply is RS, which the buyers will not demand. In order to sell excess supply, the buyers will bring down the price to OP_2 at which the demand is P_2T and the supply is P_2V. The excess demand is to the extent of VT. This excess demand will gradually push the price to the equilibirium point. As long as the supply and demand remain more or less equal, the current equilibirium price prevails in the market.

Time element in perfect competition

Marshall was the first economist to introduce the concept of time in price determination. Apart from price which influences the demand and supply of a commodity, there are certain other factors which influences the demand and supply of a commodity. One of these elements is time. Marshall divided time period into the three categories: market period, short period, and the long period.

1. Market Period: According to Marshall, it refers to a competitive market in which the commodities are perishable and supply of commodities cannot be changes. The price is determined only by the changes in demand, the length of the market period differs from commodity to commodity. For in case of certain vegetables the supply may lag behind demand by a day, while

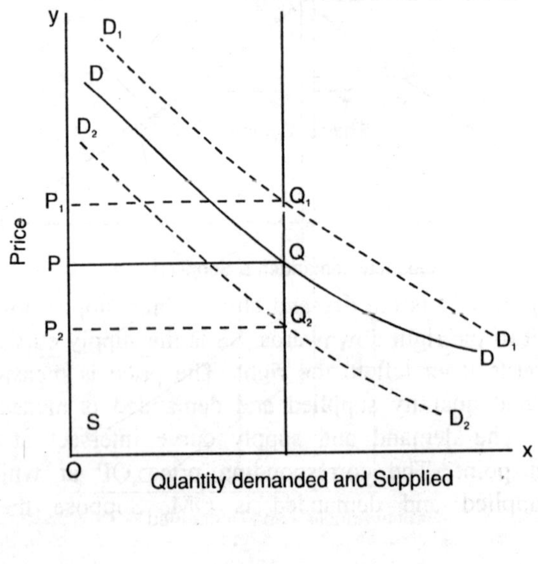

for goods like refrigerators the market period may extend for a few days. Thus market price is determined by the forces of demand and supply in the market at a point of time.

In the figure, SS is the supply curve, which is a vertical straight line the supply being fixed. DD is the demand curve and it intersects the demand curve at Q. at the point the price is OP. suppose if the demand changes to D_1D_1 on a particular day, the equilibirium point will shift to Q_1 resulting in the price increasing to OP_1. If the demand decreases to D_2D_2 as indicated in the figure, the price will fall to OP_2. It is thus noted that in the short period, the demand decides the price as the supply is not only fixed but the commodities used are perishable in nature.

2. Short period: The short period is defined as the period in which the firm is free to vary its output, to a certain extent, as it has very little time to change its scale of plant. The number of firms in the industry would be fixed, as it would be difficult for the new firms to enter and compete with the existing firms in the short period. If the demand for the commodity increases, the individual firms will increase their output with the existing capacity. Since only the variable factors can be changed and not the fixed factor. The supply curve in the short period is thus elastic and it is upward sloping.

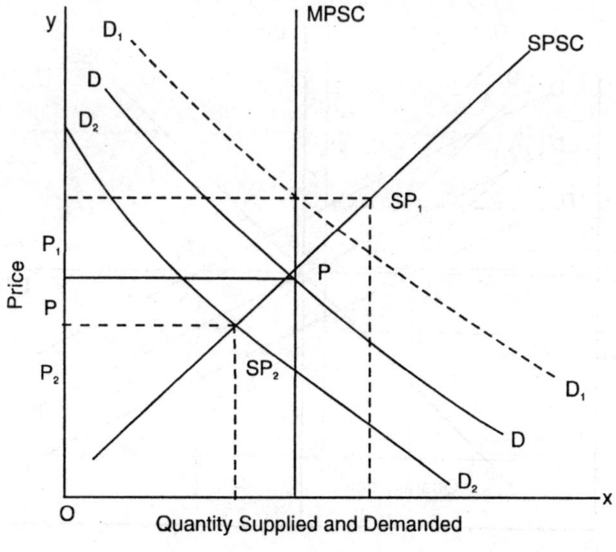

In the case of short period, the supply to some extent decides the price of the commodity, within the available stock limit and availability to stock, the supply can influence the price. At the same time, the control of stock and its influence on price depends on the demand in the future of the commodity. The determination of the short period price can be explained through a figure.

In the figure SPSC indicates the short period supply curve which is slightly elastic. A shift in the demand curve from DD to D_1D_1 means an increase in demand. When the demand increases the supply also increases to some extent, hence the price rises from P to SP_1. Similarly when the demand decreases to D_2D_2, the new price is determined at SP_2. SP_1 and SP_2 indicate the short period prices.

3. Long period: Long period is a period long enough for the firms to alter their output since they can vary their variable factors and the fixed factors. These changes allow the firms to change their supply according to the prevailing demand for their commodities in the market. New firms can enter the industry and the old can increase their existing capacity. Thus the interaction between the long period supply and demand determines the long period price. Price is determined at the point of intersection between the long run demand supply curves.

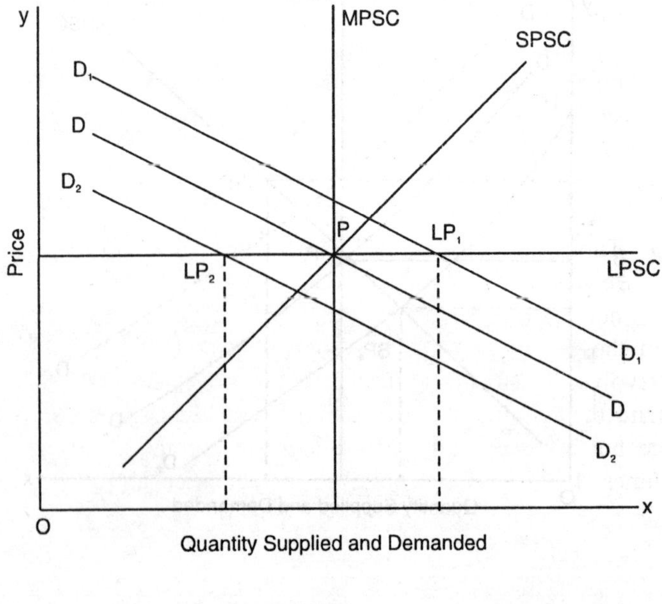

In the above figure LPSC is the long period supply curve which represents a horizontal straight line, which is perfectly elastic. This indicates that the changes in supply brings about equal changes in demand. Hence P, LP_1 and LP_2 are at the same level representing one price level. In the long run supply for ce plays a dominant role than the demand force. Thus the long run price is also referred to as normal price.

Thus it can be seen that how 'time' as a factor helps in bringing rapid changes to the market forces of demand and supply.

The normal price and market price

In the day to day business dealings the terms 'normal price' and 'market price' are used. Though both these concepts seem to be the same, yet they tend to differ in their meaning slightly.

- Market price refers to the market period price. It is the equilibirium price determined by the interaction of demand and supply. Normal price on the other hand, refers to the long period price. It is determined by the long run demand and supply of the commodity.
- The supply tends to be fixed and perfectly inelastic in the market price. But in the case of normal price, the supply tends to be fairly elastic, it has relatively a greater impact on setting an equilibirium price.
- Market price keeps fluctuating. It reflects the unstable equilibrium positions of demand and supply. Normal price on the other hand is a stable phenomenon. It represents stabilized equilibirium conditions of demand and supply. In simple words market equilibrium is temporary in nature. Where as normal price is the more or less permanent equilibirium position of the commodity.
- Though the market price is fluctuating, it is more or less related to the normal price. It tends to revolve around the normal price and tends to be equal for a moment.

In the below figure it is seen that market period price tends to revolve around the normal price. It moves up and down, but around the normal price. Sometimes it is higher than the normal price but at times it may be below the normal price and equal at times. It is thus seen both the market price and normal price

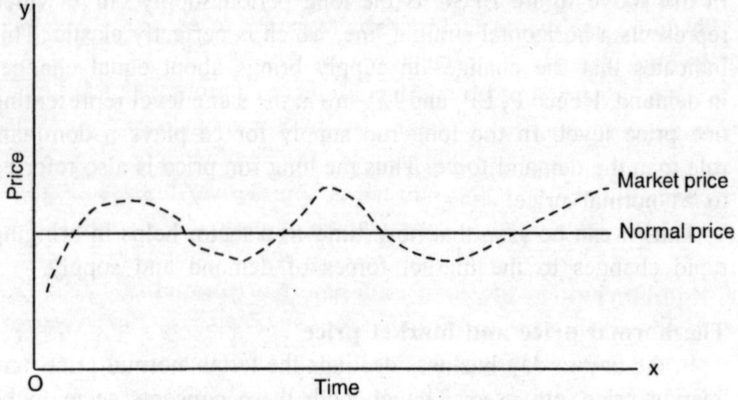

Relationship between market price and normal price

are basically the market forces namely demand and supply, but at varying degrees.

Firm and industry

In 'economics', the term 'Firm' refers to a "unit of control." Or it refers to an enterprise engaged in the production of a commodity. It is considered as a unit of control whose production has range a of commodities under production. An industry on the other hand is particular line of productive activity in which many firms are engaged in adopting its own production and price policies. The industry may consists of many firms producing the same commodity and competing. A firm is productive unit. It has no bearing either on the ownership or the controlling body. The firm is usually personified in the entrepreneur in economic analysis.

The firms in the industry have to be interdependent and they together constitute a complex group of the productive system, in which firms will be competing, and controlling different set of forces. Each firm decides the product to be produced, the nature of the product, quality of the product, and the technique of production. It also decides the quantity to be produced depending on the plant capacity, and also intensity of demand for the product and quantity offered for sale in the market. The firm also has to decide the pricing policy to be undertaken depending on the prevailing market situation. For example taking the room charges of different 5 star hotels in a particular area. The rental charges of the rooms would almost remain similar to each other or would revolve around a particular price.

An industry on the other hand refers to a group of firms engaged in the production of a specific commodity including its substitutes. Thus an industry is a set of firms producing homogenous commodities. And the industry is spread over a wider region. It is also seen that the firms use a common raw material.

Equilibirium of the firm under perfect competition

A firm is said to be in equilibrium, when it has reached its profitable position where it can maximize its profit. A firm is said to be in equilibirium when it has no motive to change its organization or scale of production. An industry on the other hand is said to be equilibirium when there is no tendency for the firms composing it, either to increase or to decrease.

The concept of equilibirium is a condition of maximum profit, i.e., the firms aims at maximum profit and will not be happy with the existing normal profit. There exists a distinction between the normal and supernormal profit of the firms. Normal profit is the minimum reasonable level of profit, which the entrepreneur must get in the long run, so that he is induced to reinvest in his business. It is considered as the least possible reward, which in the long run must be earned by the entrepreneur as compensation for his organizational services. Thus profit is nothing but the total revenue minus the total cost. Supernormal profits on the other hand refer to the reward for bearing uncertainties and unpredictable risks of business. At times supernormal profits are earned due to the extraordinary efficiency on the part of the entrepreneur. According to Koutsoyinnis, maximization of profits refers to the 'profit which is not included in the cost items of the firm, which is above the normal rate of return on capital and remuneration for the organizational and risk bearing functions of the entrepreneur'.

Essential conditions

In a perfectly competitive situation, all firms obtain the same price for the commodity, for their product. To obtain the equilibirium the firms will try to equalize marginal revenue to marginal cost.

Marginal cost will be a 'U' shaped curve. The marginal revenue curve is a straight line parallel to the x axis. The firms will thus come to equilibirium at that level of output at which the MC equals the MR and the MC curve cuts the MR curve from below. Thus for the firms to be in equilibirium two conditions have to be fulfilled viz.,

1. MR = MC = Price
2. MC curve must cut the MR curve from below at the point of equilibirium or (MC > MR) MC must be greater than MR.

The short run marginal revenue of the firm depends on the price of the product. The short run equilibirium price is determined in the market by the intersection of the demand and supply curves shown below.

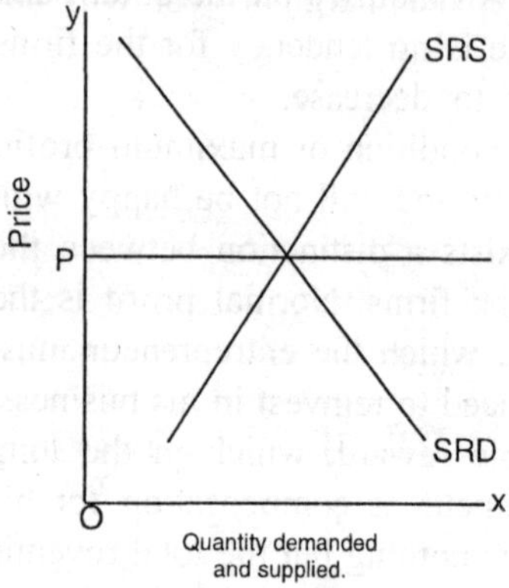

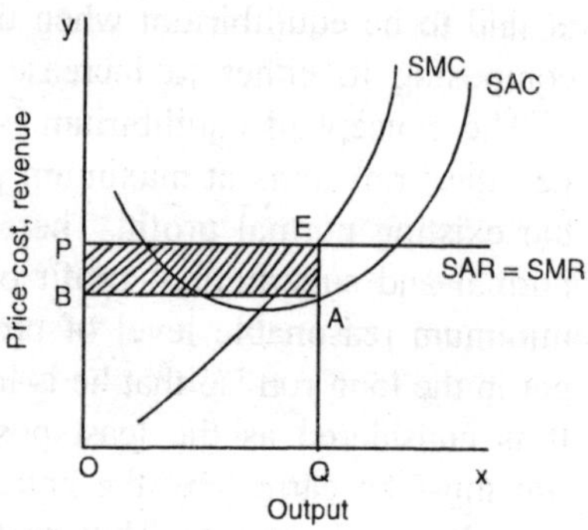

From the firms point of view, the demand for the product is purely elastic. Thus in the short period, OP is the price, and the demand curve is a horizontal straight line, corresponding to which the short run average revenue and the short run marginal revenue are depicted.

In the figure E is the equilibirium point, at which the SMC curve is equal to the SMR curve. OQ is the equilibirium level of output determined by the firm in the short run. Since the area under the average revenue and cost curves measure total revenue and total cost, the difference between the two show profit. The per unit profit is PB. The total profit earned by the firm is profit per unit multiplied by the number of units produced and sold. Thus the shaded area PEAB represents maximum profits. All firms will be earning supernormal profits in the short run. This is one of the conditions for the firms to be in equilibirium.

The other condition is that marginal revenue and marginal cost must intersect the MR curve from below. This is illustrated through the figure below. In the figure MR is the marginal revenue curve and MC is the marginal cost line. The marginal cost curve cuts the MR curve at two places At point A the marginal cost cuts the marginal revenue but from above. At this point OM is the quantity produced at OP price. At this point the marginal revenue obtained is greater than the marginal cost, which induces the firms to produce. At point E the marginal cost curve again cuts the marginal revenue curve but from below. This is point where MR = MC, where the firms obtain total profit. Beyond the point E, even if the firms desires to produce, the marginal cost will be greater than the marginal revenue.

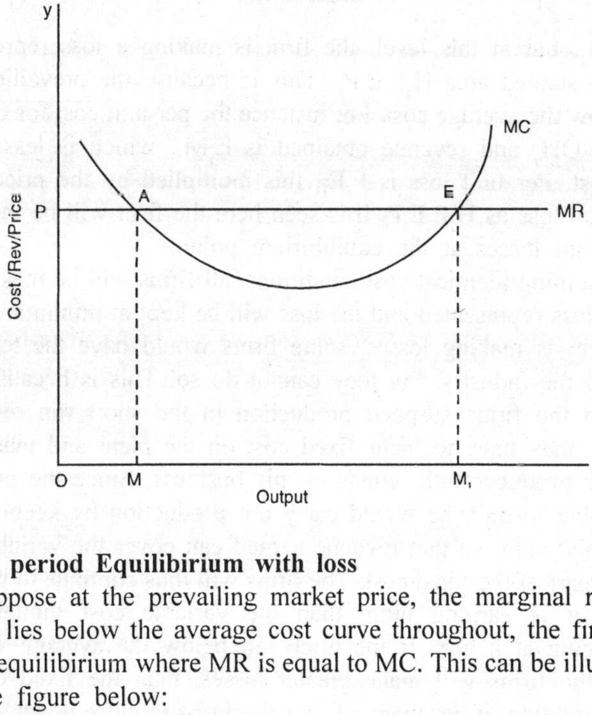

Short period Equilibirium with loss

Suppose at the prevailing market price, the marginal revenue curve lies below the average cost curve throughout, the firm will be in equilibirium where MR is equal to MC. This can be illustrated in the figure below:

In the figure, At E_1, MR = MC and the equilibirium output

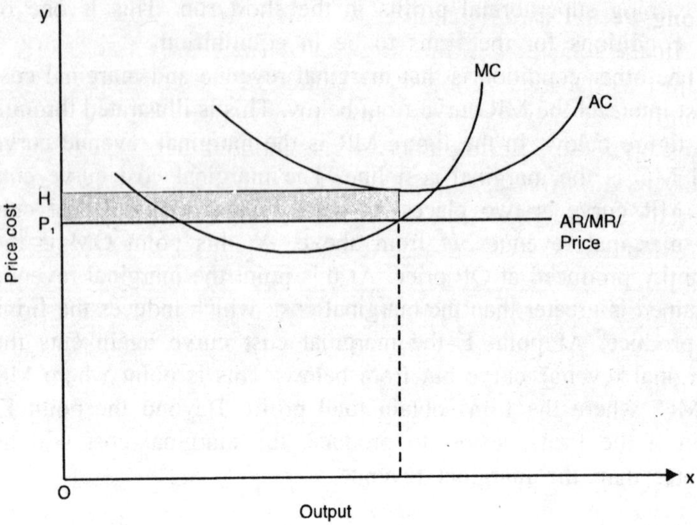

is OM_1, but at this level, the firm is making a loss represented by the shaded area $H_1F_1E_1P_1$. This is because the prevailing OP_1 is below the average cost. For instance the per unit cost for OM_1out put is OH_1 and revenue obtained is E_1M_1, which is lesser than the cost. Per unit loss is F_1E_1, this multiplied by the price gives the total loss as $H_1F_1E_1P$. It is seen here the firm will be incurring minimum losses at the equilibirium point.

Assuming identical cost conditions, all firms will be making the exact loss represented and the loss will be kept at minimum. Since the firm is making losses, some firms would have the tendency to quit the industry, but they cannot do so. This is because even though the firms suspend production in the short run owing to losses, they have to incur fixed cost on the plant and machinery till the producer fully winds up his business. Since the producer is unable to quit, he would carry out production by keeping loss at a minimum, so that revenue earned can cover the variable cost and a part of the fixed cost. The firms will thus continue to produce when it is earning more than the variable cost though it is producing at a loss. If the price fall below the average variable cost, the firms will make greater losses, than the fixed cost. In this condition, it becomes safe for the firms to close down in order to prevent further losses.

Long Period Equilibirium

In the long period, the firms can change their fixed cost and adjust to the long period normal price of the commodity. In the long period, there will more entry of new firms into the industry, thus bringing down the price of the commodities. The firms will only earn only normal profits at the equilibirium point. There are certain conditions, which hold good for the long run equilibirium:

1. Marginal cost is equal to cost
2. Price = average cost.

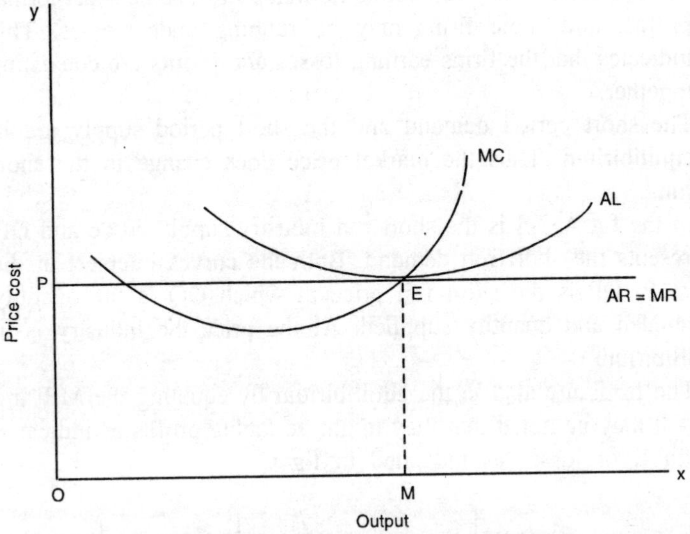

The figure above explains the long run equilibirium of the firm under perfect competition. The long run equilibirium output is OM. The firm is earning just normal profit at OP price. If the price is less than OP the tendency will be to exit from the firm and this will again push up the price. So in the equilibirium, OP will be the price and marginal cost will be equal to average cost and the average revenue and marginal revenue curve will be tangent to the long run average cost curve making the point of tangency at the lower most point of the LAC curve. This indicates the firm is operating at the optimum level with the minimum cost conditions.

Equilibirium of the Industry under Perfect Competition

An industry is said to be in equilibirium when the industry's demand is equal to the industry's supply. There are three conditions to be satisfied for an industry to be in equilibirium in the short run:

1. The individual firms should not have any tendency to expand. When each individual firm produces an output at which MR is equal to MC, no existing firms will vary their output.
2. It needed be necessary for all the firms to earn profits in the short run. Some may be earning normal profits, some supernormal profits, and some firms may be running under losses. This indicates that the firms earning losses and profits are coexisting together.
3. The short period demand and the short period supply are in equilibirium. Thus the market price does change in the short run.

In the fig A, SS is the short run industry supply curve and DD represents the short run demand. Both the curves intersect at the point E. OP is the short run price at which OQ is the quantity demanded and quantity supplied. At the price the industry is in equilibirium.

The firms are also in the equilibirium by equating the MR and MC. It may be noted that they might be facing profits as indicated in fig B or losses as indicated in fig C.

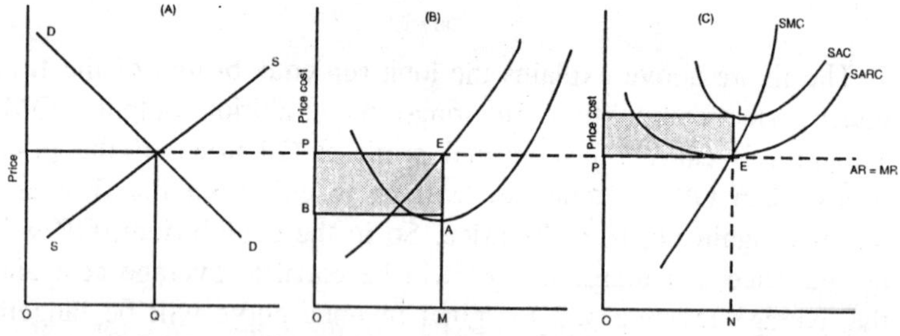

Output

Industry & Tirms Equilibirium

Long Run Equilibirium of the Industry

In the long run period the industry attains equilibirium with the supply and demand conditions coming to a equilibirium position.

The industry reaches an equilibirium position in the long run under the following conditions:

1. All firms in the long run will be producing at an equilibirium level by equating their marginal cost with the long run marginal revenue. The aggregate of their output constitutes the total supply of the industry.
2. There should no new entry into the industry.
3. The firms must be producing at a level where LAR= LAC.
4. All firms should earn only normal profits, if some firms are earning supernormal profits that would induce new firms to enter into competition.

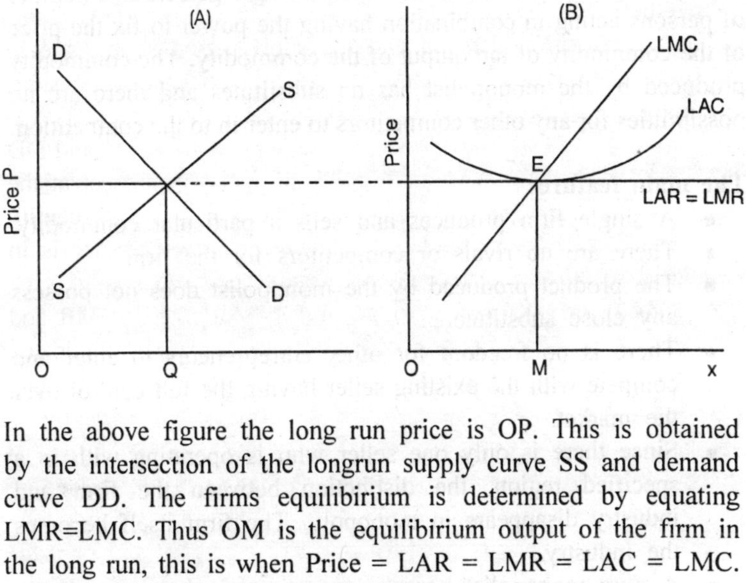

In the above figure the long run price is OP. This is obtained by the intersection of the longrun supply curve SS and demand curve DD. The firms equilibirium is determined by equating LMR=LMC. Thus OM is the equilibrium output of the firm in the long run, this is when Price = LAR = LMR = LAC = LMC. The firms enjoys only normal profits.

Consequences of Perfect Competition

The economic consequences of perfectly competitive situation would be that:

- It ensures maximum welfare of the people as a whole. Each factor of production is utilized where it is best suited.
- Each consumer buys commodities of his own liking, as he is free to choose from a range of commodities whose price is uniform.

- The firms expand their output till a position where they can reduce their average cost of production. Beyond this point any increase in production will only increase the cost of production and reduce profits.

9.4. MONOPOLY

Monopoly is defined a market structure where there is only one seller who controls the entire market supply. The term 'monopolist' is derived from the greek word 'mono' meaning 'single' and 'polist' meaning 'seller'. Thus it indicates absence of competition. An extreme situation of perfect competition, monopoly is also defined as a condition of production in which a single person or a number of persons acting in combination having the power to fix the price of the commodity of the output of the commodity. The commodity produced by the monopolist has no substitutes and there are no possibilities for any other competitors to enter in to the competition.

The main features

- A single firm produces and sells a particular commodity.
- There are no rivals or competitors for the firm.
- The product produced by the monopolist does not possess any close substitute.
- There is no freedom for other entrepreneurs to enter and compete with the existing seller having the full control over the market.
- Since there is only one seller who is operating with in a specified region, the distinction between the firm and industry disappears in monopoly. The firm itself becomes the industry.
- A pure monopolist has no immediate rival due to certain barriers. There are legal, technological, economic are a few obstacles, which block the entry of the firms.
- A monopolist is price maker and not a price taker. In fact, his price fixing power is absolute. He is in a position to change the price between his buyers. Thus in a monopoly situation there will be price differentials.

Types of monopoly:

- ***Discriminating monopoly:*** When the monopolist changes the price of the product between one buyer and another, such a situation is known as discriminating monopoly. The monopolist also changes the prices between the markets.
- ***Simple monopoly:*** It is a situation where the single producer a commodity has a rare substitute. In simple monopoly the monopolist will have some substitute, but in the economic analysis it is understood that a monopoly firm produces a commodity having no close substitutes.
- ***Pure monopoly:*** A phenomenon specific to the public sector. When a particular sector takes the exclusive privilege of producing a commodity, which is being exclusively produced by that sector. In pure monopoly there are no substitutes to the commodity.

Monopoly equilibirium (price and output determination)

A monopolist is a price maker, and not a price taker and his power is absolute in the market. He has total control over the market supply, but he cannot charge a higher price than the said price. This is because he may obtain a lesser demand for his commodities at a higher price. The principle of profit maximization is that the monopolist will maximize his net revenue by keeping the marginal cost and marginal revenue at the same level. The profit maximization formula of MR = MC holds well here. The monopolist will go on producing till additional units of output sold add more to the revenue than the cost. He will stop at a point beyond which additional units cost him more than the revenue realized.

The equilibirium of the monopoly is explained through a figure below.

In the figure, the MR curve lies below the AR curve and it appears to be a steeper curve than the AR curve. This is because since AR is falling, the extra units sold would fetch lesser revenue in the market. E is determined by the intersection of the MR curve and MC curve, so that MC = MR. Thus, OM out put is produced at OP price. The price is determined by drawing a perpendicular AM which intercepts the demand curve (AR curve) at point A.

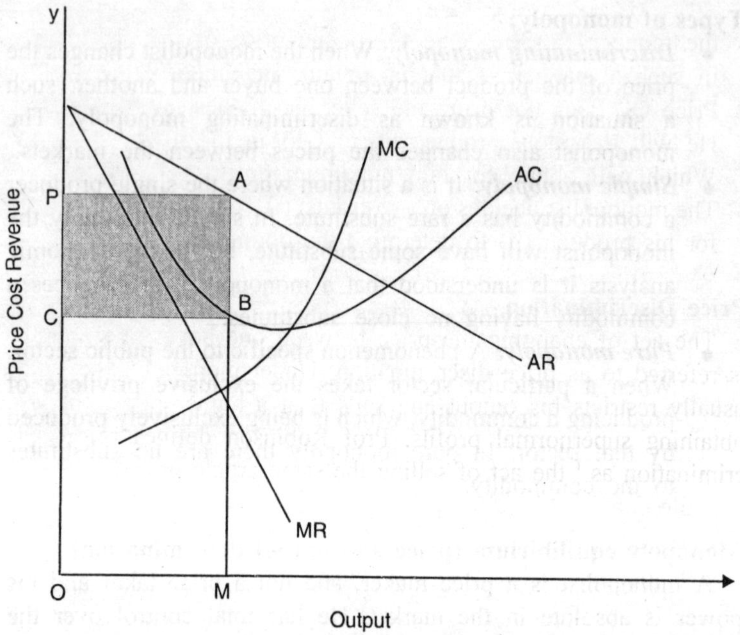

Once the out put is decided, the price is determined automatically in relation to the given demand curve. To maximize his profits, the monopolist adopts the rationale of equating MC with MR. When the equilibirium output is decided at the point of equality between MC and MR, the price is automatically determined in relation to the demand for the product. In the figure it is seen that the monopolist will not charge a price higher than OP. If he does, he will not be able to sell OM output. He would not like to lower the price either because that will reduce his profit.

Thus when OP price is charged, OM output is sold; the monopolist obtains a maximum profit, which is represented by the shaded rectangle PABC. This is termed as monopoly profit. The monopoly equilibirium output is determined at the falling path of the AC curve, which means that the monopolist restricts the output before producing it at the optimum level.

Features of the Monopoly Price

1. It is the highest price possible. Any price above the equilibirium indicates that monopolist will sell only a less commodity. Hence

the monopolist takes care to fix the price of the commodity in such a manner so that he obtains maximum profits.

2. Price OP does not bring the seller the highest average profit. He will definitely produce up to OM in the given situation. Which will obtain for him maximum profit.
3. The monopolist decides on two fronts: (i) To determine the price for his product. (ii) to determine the optimum level of output.

Price Discrimination

The act of changing the price between one buyer and another is referred to as price discrimination. Under monopoly, the seller usually restricts his output and sells it at a higher price, thereby obtaining supernormal profits. Prof Robinson defines price discrimination as ' the act of selling the same article produced under a single control at different prices to different consumers'. It may also be defined as 'the sales of technically similar products at prices which are not proportional to marginal cost'.

Forms of Price Discrimination

Personal discrimination: When different prices are charged to the different buyers, it is known personal discrimination. For example while buying note books, an ordinary note book may cost around Rs. 10, but on the other hand the deluxe notebook may cost the customer Rs. 20. Another example would be that of the services of a doctor. He may charge the rich patient a different fee, but a poor patient may be charged less. The doctor's fees differ here due the different status of his patients.

Locational discrimination: When price discrimination exists depending on the area of selling, it is known as local discrimination. For instance, when middle class consumers frequently visit an area for shopping the prices in that area would be different than in a area where the richer class visit. A firm may also discriminate between the domestic and local market.

Size discrimination: When discrimination is resorted due to the differences in size, packaging, etc., it is known as size discrimination. Similar commodities may be priced differently by making minor changes like changing the shape, size, changing brand names and changing the packaging style. For instance, if the cost of a dress is Rs. 450, the producer may slightly change the name by branding it as 'made of imported yarn' or 'export quality' and thus may price is as Rs. 700.

Trade discrimination: Also called use discrimination, the monopolist here will charge different prices for different types of uses for the same commodity. For instance, the charges of electricity for domestic use is slightly high. It is less for industries, this is because the consumption by the industries is more than that of the household.

Price discrimination: When different prices are charged for the same commodity. It is known as price discrimination. The monopolist does this in order to gain abnormal profits.

Conditions Necessary for Price Discrimination

Though the monopolist earns supernormal profits by changing the price of his commodity between one buyer and another, it is seen he cannot resort to this discriminatory practice all the time. Discrimination can work only when certain conditions are fulfilled. They are:

1. ***Separate markets:*** Markets are basically divided in to sub-markets. Each sub markets have their own identity, so that they do not have connection with the other. They might be separated by distance, in this case the prices of the same commodities can differ between each of these sub markets.
2. ***Product differentiation:*** Through minor changes, similar products can be varied by changing their size, colour, packaging etc. Thus these products can be sold to different categories at varying prices.
3. ***Distance and trade barriers:*** When commodities are separated by distance or trade barriers, price discrimination may be resorted to. For example, if a monopolist is supplying his commodities in two places. In a place where the distance involves less of transport he might charge a less price than in a place which involves more transport cost. The monopolist may charge a lesser price for his commodities in a place where the taxes are low and charge a high price where he taxed high.
4. ***Non-transferability of goods:*** Some goods cannot be transferred between one buyer and another. In personal services, price

discrimination is easily resorted to. For instance, a doctor may wish to discriminate between his rich and poor patient.

5. ***Consumers psychology:*** Some consumers have a feeling that buying a particular commodity in a certain area has more durability, and they do buy the commodity even if it is highly priced. Knowing the consumers' preference the monopolist may charge a high price for commodity in that area, thereby earning supernormal profits.
6. ***Legal sanctions:*** In some cases price discrimination is legally sanctioned. For instance if electricity is misused in households without prior permission, the customer is liable for penalties.

When is Price Discrimination Profitable?

Price discrimination basically depends on the nature of elasticity of demand. It will be profitable only under certain conditions: *A*. elasticity of demand should be different in the two markets. *B*. The cost of keeping the various markets and sub-markets with discriminatory prices should not be very much.

The monopolist can increase the prices in a market where there is a inelastic situation i.e., the demand for the commodities should vary with an increase in price. In market where the demand for his commodities is elastic, the monopolist should not change the price rapidly.

Pricing under discriminating monopoly: The figure illustrates the revenue curves of the two sub-markets A and B and the aggregate market. In the sub-market A AR_1 is the demand or the average revenue curve of the market. In the sub market B, AR_2 is the demand curve or the average curve of the sub market B. In the sub market A, the demand is inelastic in nature and in the sub market B, it is elastic. In the two submarkets the MR_1 and MR_2 are the marginal revenues curves which fall below the average curves. The figure on the extreme right is the aggregate market curve, which shows the aggregate revenue curves. The total average revenue curve is AAR, and the average revenue curve AMR. According to the figure AR_1+AR_2 = AAR; MR_1 + MR_2 = AMR. Since the output is under a single control, the marginal cost in shown in the aggregate figure. The level of production is determined at a point where MR = MC. In the total market the aggregate MR curve cuts the MC curve at E, and the total output is OM. This level of the output has to be sold in the two markets. To find out, a parallel line from E is drawn towards the x axis. This line indicating the marginal cost of the two markets cuts the marginal revenue of the two sub markets at point E_2 and E_1.

The equilibirium condition in sub market A lies at E_1 where the quantity of commodity should be OM_1. Similarly the equilibirium, point in the sub market B lies at E_2, where the marginal cost level meets the marginal revenue of that market. The corresponding quantity is OM_2. thus OM_1 quantity will be sold in the sub market A and OM_2 will be sold in the sub market B. At the equilibirium point E_1, the price of the commodity will P_1M_1. in the sub market B, at the equilibirium point, average revenue is P_2M_2, so the price is P_2M_2. Thus the monopolist producing OM quantity will sell OM_1 in sub market A at P_1 price and OM_2 quantity in sub market 2 at P_2 price. It is thus seen that in the sub market A the price is high and in the sub market B the price charged is low.

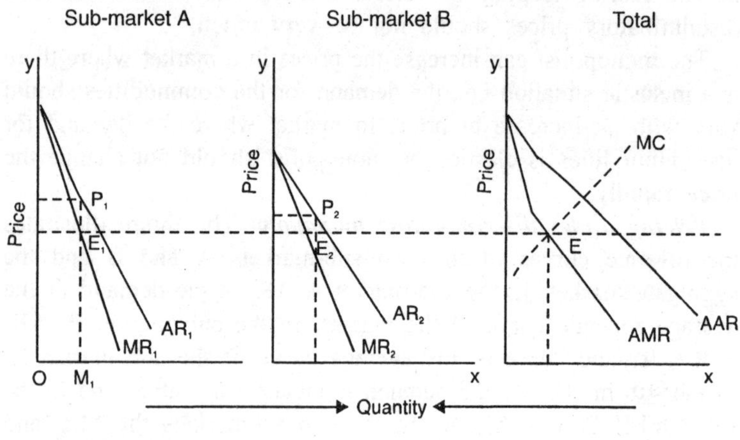

Dumping

Dumping implies the act of changing the price between the home market and the foreign market. Haberler defines dumping as 'the sale of a good abroad at a price which is lower than the selling price of the same good at the same time and in the same circumstances at home, taking account of differences in transport costs'.

The monopolist has a good demand in the domestic or the home market and he may have not such a monopoly power in the foreign market, thus he tries to decrease the price of his commodities in the foreign market, so that he obtains a good demand and in the home market he might not decrease the price. The rationale behind dumping is that it enables the exporter to compete in the foreign market and capture the market by selling at a low price, even at times below the cost of production. The higher domestic price helps to subsidize a portion of foreign price which helps promote exports.

Dumping helps the producer to widen the size of the foreign market, for his products. It reduces his investment risks when the launch of the product is on a large scale. The export earnings also enable to promote home industries, and dumping also increases the quality of the product making it more competitive at the international level.

However the success of dumping depends on the following conditions:

- The producer must produce quality goods, which can withhold international competitiveness.
- He must possess a degree of monopoly power in the home market.
- There should be a clear demarcation between the home and foreign market, in terms of distance, tariffs, customs, language and currency.
- Price discrimination is profitable only when the two different markets have different elasticities of demand, it becomes difficult to differentiate the price when the two markets are operating under identical demand conditions.
- The producer must be able to capture the foreign market effectively with out incurring a loss.

9.5. DUOPOLY

It is type of imperfect market in which there are only two sellers producing an identical product in the market. Augustin Cournot, a French economist, was the first economist to develop the model of duopoly. In a duopoly situation, each seller may sell an identical product or a differentiated product. Duopoly may be broadly classified into:

1. Duopoly with product differentiation: Here the producers may be producing the same product, but there may be minor differences in packaging, size, colour, shape etc. When there is product differentiation each seller may have his own customers for the product and is not afraid of this rival.

2. Duopoly without product differentiation: When similar products are produced by the competing duopolists it is known as duopoly without product differentiation. In such a situation each seller cannot ignore the price and output of the rival in the market. In the event of a good understanding between the two sellers, each seller tries to out wit the other, which results in cut throat competition between the sellers. This leads to a situation where price may fall to the level of the competitive price at which price = cost, the profit in this case will be normal.

Under duopoly the price is indeterminate, it may be fluctuating between the monopoly price and competitive price depending upon the degree of understanding and misunderstanding.

9.6. OLIGOPOLY

Oligopoly is derived from two Greek words 'Oligos' meaning 'a few' and 'pollein', 'to sell'. Thus Oligopoly refers to that form of market where there are few sellers producing either an identical product or a differentiated product. According to professor Stigler, 'Oligopoly is a situation in which a firm bases its market policy in part on the expected behaviour of a few close rivals'. Thus it is a market form where there are few sellers who are interdependent of each others survival in the market. Their number is beyond two and below nine. Feller thus defines oligopoly as 'competition among the few'. It can also stated as, 'a situation where a few large firms compete against each other and there is an element of interdependence'. The best examples of oligopoly markets are petrol, lubricants.

Classification of the oligopoly market

The oligopoly market can be classified in to the following groups:

1. *Product differentiation:* If the products in the industry are homogenous in nature, it is called perfect or pure oligopoly. If the industry produces more or less similar products, which

are close substitutes it is called imperfect or differentiated oligopoly.

2. ***Entry of firms:*** If the firms are free to enter into competition, it is open oligopoly, if the firms find restriction in entering into competition it is known as closed oligopoly.
3. ***Price leadership:*** The oligopoly can be classified into partial oligopoly or full oligopoly depending on the presence or the absence of the price leader. Full oligopoly refers to a situation when no firms act as a leader. Partial oligopoly is when there exists a firm which acts as a leader controlling the prices and dominating the market.
4. ***Agreement between firms:*** Instead of competing with each other when the firms arrive at a tacit understanding and follow a common price policy, it is called collusive oligopoly. Alternatively if the firms follow their independent price policy without a common understanding it is known as non-collusive oligopoly.

Characteristic Feature of Oligopoly

Price rigidity: In a oligopoly market each firm sticks to its own price. This is because it is in constant fear of retaliation from the rival firms. No firm would indulge in price cutting as it would eventually lead to a price war with no benefit to anyone. Price can be kept constant without any agreement also.

Element of monopoly: In oligopoly market, where there is the existence of few firms, there is the monopoly element present. Each firms controls a large share of the market, with a differentiated, leading it to become a small monopolist.

Few Sellers: An oligopoly market is characterized by a group of few sellers who either sell a similar product or a differentiated product.

Lack of uniformity: Products of the oligopolist though would be similar, would be differentiated with small differences in changing packages, size, shape of the product thus, making it appear different.

Cross Elasticity: The commodities sold by the oligopolist have a degree of cross elasticity. For instance if firm X is selling a commodity at Rs. 30 and firm Y is selling a similar product at

Rs. 35. now if Firm Y decreases its price suddenly to Rs. 25, firm Y will have more demand. Hence X would retaliate by reducing the price from Rs. 30 to even Rs. 20. Thus each firm in oligopoly is conscious of retaliation, and would react accordingly.

Lack of certainty: Lack of certainty is another characteristic feature of the oligopoly market. They have two conflicting motives: (1) To remain in the market. (2) To maximise profits. The firms know their interdependence in the market and they also realise the importance of mutual cooperation. At times, to obtain mutual gains, they collude with each other. On the other hand when the desire of each firm is to make maximum profits, and obtain maximum market for their goods, they react in an adverse situation creating an unhealthy competitive environment. Thus to pursue their ends they act and react to the variation in price and other factors, resulting in a uncertainty situation.

Interdependence: The firms have a high degree of interdependence between themselves. As the number of firms are few, a change in price and output by a firm will directly affect the other firm which would retaliate by changing their own price and output likewise. Hence to prevent a un healthy competition, like a price war or cut throat competition, the firms depend more or less on each other as far as price fixation is concerned.

Selling cost: Advertising and selling cost play an important role in an oligopoly market. A direct effect of interdependence and indeterminateness of demand of various firms in oligopoly is the enormous selling cost incurred by the competing firms. To increase the demand for the product each firms will employ various advertisement techniques, effecting the selling cost to increase. According to Baumol, "advertising can be a life-and-death matter where a firm which fails to keep up with the advertising budget of its competitors may find its customers drifting off to rival products".

Price Leadership under Oligopoly

The act of fixing the price by a dominant firm is known as price leadership. Referred to as the 'most important form of imperfect collusion', Burns refers to it, "if changes are usually or always inaugurated by the same firm and usually or always followed with similar price changes by other sellers, price competition may be said to involve price leadership".

Price Leadership may be Broadly Classified as

1. Dominant firm price leadership
2. Collusive price leadership
3. Barometric leadership

1. Dominant firm price leadership: In this situation it is assumed that there is one large firm and many small firms. The dominant firm fixes the price and the small firms act as price takers. This type of price leadership is also referred to as partial monopoly, as the dominant firm wields more or less a monopoly power.

2. Collusive price leadership: This situation may emerge out of explicit or a tacit collusion. Here the leader may be the largest firm in the group or the one with the lowest cost. If the firm is large, it is in the interest of the small firms to follow the price change initiated by the dominant firm. Alternatively, if the firm has a low cost of production, which enables it to lower the price the other firms have to follow suit.

3. Barometric Leadership: The firm assumes the leadership, it acts as a 'barometer', reflecting changing market conditions or cost that require a change in price. Due to certain external factors the leadership role may also fall on a small firm, which might be an efficient one. The firm may in a position to judge the changes in demand and cost conditions and fix the price which the suits the group best. This form of leadership may be short lived due to the aggressive policy of the dominant firms.

The price leadership helps in preventing stiff competition between rivals. Cut throat competition can be avoided. Interdependence of the firms on one another helps in reducing the uncertainty linked with actions and counteractions of the rival firms.

Kinked Demand Curve

Paul Sweezy propounded this model. It represents a condition in which the firm has no incentive to increase the price or decrease it. It keeps the price rigid at a certain level. It believes the firms won't change the price if it increases its price and they would follow suit if it decreases the price. Hence it maintains the current price. Only in crucial situations like changes in the cost or demand the firm would think of changing the price. The model is explained through the figure below.

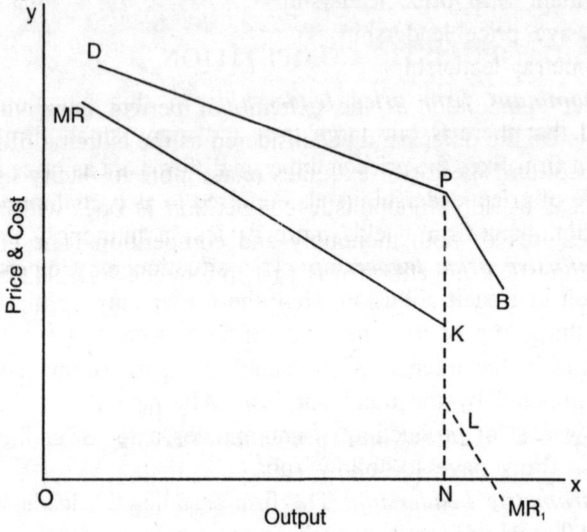

In the figure, the demand curve is divided into two segments- the relatively elastic segment, the relatively inelastic segment. P is the price at which the firm is selling the product by producing ON units. Above the price P the anticipated demand will be DP, where curve is elastic. Below the price P the anticipated demand will be PB which is inelastic. This shows that when the firm increases the price beyond P and if the other firms are maintaining the same price, the demand for the firm's product would fall. Hence the demand curve appears elastic (DP portion). The total revenue and profit of the firm would be reduced.

On the other hand if the firm decreases the price, the demand curve becomes less elastic and the demand curve is shown as PB. At this level, the marginal revenue curve is shown as MR_1. When the demand curve is DP the marginal revenue is positive. When the demand curve is PB, the marginal revenue becomes negative. When the firm sees no scope for profit or loss, the firms fixes the price at PN, which becomes rigid.

An important feature of the kinked demand curve is that there is a gap or discontinuity in MR curve below the point of kink. KL shows the gap of discontinuity between MR and MR_1. This gap will depend on the elasticity of demand above and below the kink. This gap will be larger if the elasticity is greater above the kink and inelasticity is also greater below the kink.

9.7. MONOPOLISTIC COMPETITION

Perfect competition is the extreme of perfect competition, monopoly on the other hand is considered as the extreme of imperfect competition. These two extremes relate more to theory than to the practical world. Monopolistic competition is one, which exhibits the features of both monopoly and competition. The concept of monopolistic competition was first introduced by E.H.Chamberlin and Mrs Joan Robinson, who refuted the concept of perfect competition.

Monopolistic competition refers to a market situation in which there is keen competition, which neither pure nor perfect. Thus monopolistic competition is a mixture of competition and a certain degree of monopoly power. It refers to a market situation in which many producers produce, goods which are close substitutes of one another. Monopolistic competition thus indicates a market where there a large number of few sellers who are either selling the same or a differentiated product. The present business world exhibits a trend, which is more related to the monopolistic competition. From a smallest and simplistic commodity to the very sophisticated commodity, each commodity has to face severe competition from the market. This type of competition exists mostly in the service sector, retail trade, manufacturing, etc.

FEATURES OF MONOPOLISTIC COMPETITION

1. Existence of large number of firms: Monopolistic competition is characterised by a group of large sellers selling more or less a homogenous product. This leads to a competition among them. There are no possibilities of firms acting in collusion because of the large number of small sellers. Each firm will be acting independently on the basis of product differentiation and the firm determine their own price and output. Examples would be that of consumer products like soaps, tooth paste etc., which come out in large number with different brand names.

Since the number is quite large, an individual's supply is only a small percentage of the entire market supply. It has limited control over the market price. In determining its own price and production policy the firms can afford to ignore their rivals reaction.

2. Product differentiation: The most distinguishing feature of monopolistic competition is product differentiation. Though the products may be similar, their colour, size, packaging etc., will be changed allowing them to have their own price fixed. In this way the producer exhibits monopolistic power over his customers. It is found that greater the product differentiation, greater is the monopoly power.

Product differentiation can be brought in different ways. It may be by using different quality of the raw material, difference in workman ship, durability etc., product differentiation may also be effected by customers who obtain some benefits, with the sale of the product and also by effective advertising.

Thus product differentiation is done through: (a) physical difference, (b) quality difference, (c) prize offers etc. The ultimate of these firms is to obtain a large market for themselves and also to attract the customer.

3. Large number of Buyers: There are large buyers in this market. Since they are placed with a wide range of products with different brands, and different prices, they have a right to choose a product of their own choice. Hence in a monopolistic competitive situation the consumer will buy his products out of choice and not chance.

4. Free entry and free exit: Under this type of competition, there is no restriction placed for firms either to enter into the competition, or to exit from it. This makes the competition stiffer as a large number of firms produce commodities with close substitutes.

5. Selling cost: Since there are minor variation in the product produced, and the group has a large number, the sellers to attract their customers resort to various forms of sales promotion methods, which increases their investment cost. Selling costs are thus costs, which are meant for basically promoting the product, through advertising and other marketing methods. This is basically done to capture the market and to have large customers. The demand curve faced by the firm is down ward sloping. Hence, at a given price, to sell more quantity of a good, an upward shift or increase in demand curve is essential. A firm through advertisement and sales promotion efforts achieves this upward shift or increase in demand for the product.

*6. **Two dimensional competition:*** The competition has two faces. (i) Price competition — they compete with each other with regard to fixing the price of their commodities. (ii) Non-price competition — here the competition rests on changing the product with minor product differences. They also resort to heavy expenditure on advertisement and sales promotion to market their own products, indirectly affecting the sales of the rivals.

Equilibirium of the under monopolistic competition (short run)

Price and out determination under monopolistic competition is governed by the cost and revenue curves of the firm. The average revenue curve of the firm will be a sloping down curve, the curve will not too steep because, the demand under monopolistic competition will be much more sensitive to small changes in price as any fall in price ensures more customers. Similarly, any rise in price will drive out many customers from the firm to demand the product of the other firms. Thus the AR curve will be a flatter curve and the MR curve will lie below it.

In the short run the firm can adopt its own price policy with least consideration of the price of others in the market, the main aim being to maximize profits. The figure shows the equilibirium of the firm in the short run.

The short period marginal cost and average cost curves are shown as SMC and SAC. The MR curve slopes below the AR curve. The equilibirium point is determined at point E, where MR = MC. The equilibirium output is OM. The price of the product is fixed at OP. The difference between average cost and average revenue is RQ. The output is OM. The supernormal profits earned

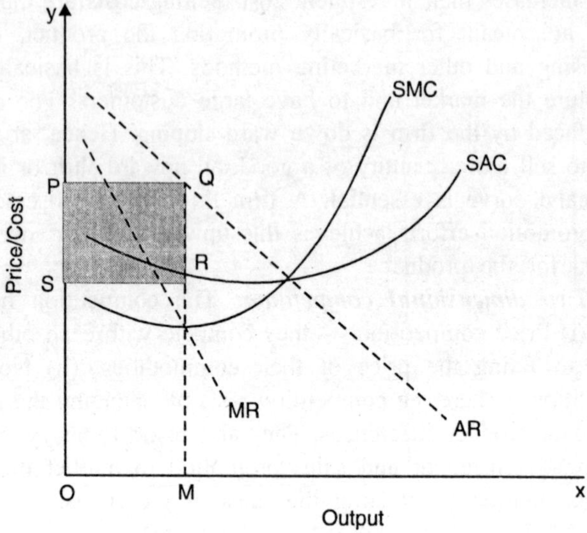

is indicated by the shaded rectangle PQRS. Such profits are possible in the short run when there are no rivals to closely substituted commodities. Which would obtain the supernormal profits of the existing firms.

Long run equilibirium

The abnormal profits made by the firms in the short run will attract new firms, in to the business. On account of the rival's entry the demand curve faced by the firm will shift to the origin and it will become more elastic. This will compel the existing firms to reduce the prices of their products. As a result of keen competition, price will fall. The Average revenue curve becomes tangent to the average cost curve. The abnormal situation will be removed. This is explained in the figure below.

LPAR and LPMR are the long run average revenue and long run marginal revenue curves. LPMC and LPAC are the long run marginal and average cost curves. The point E is the equilibirium where MR = MC and the output is OM. At the equilibirium output the average revenue, the price is OP, where the firm obtains only normal profits. The rectangle OPKM is the total revenue as well the total cost, so the firms earns only normal profit in the long

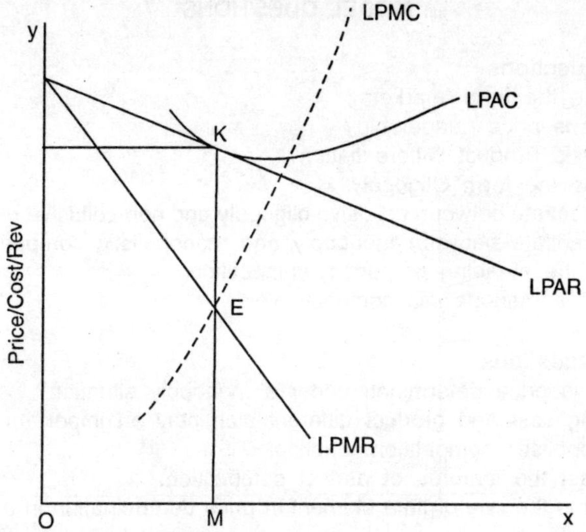

run. The existing competitors in the long run will be producing similar products, and their economic profits will be competed away. At OP price, which is equal to the average cost, the firm attains equilibirium and it breaks even. Since the LAR curve is tangent to the LAC curve at point P, any output less than OM indicates that AR < AC, indicating a loss. Another point to be noted is that in the long run the demand tends to becomes more elastic. This is because, in the long run the firms tend to produce similar products . When the products become very close substitutes of each other, the demand curve becomes more elastic.

The external environment also plays a role in affecting the functioning of the business. In the hotel industry, for example it may not be a single star hotel which is functioning in the entire city, it may have different groups of star hotels. Hence it has to be tactful in its operation—whether it fixing the price of its rooms, the different types of the accommodation it provides, the different types of cuisine it offers and the price it charges for the same. It has to have a fair knowledge of its rivals functioning and thereby act accordingly. Hence it is seen here that the understanding of the competitive market situation helps the firm- what ever be its production line, to survive the competition and to expand its operation in an effective manner.

MODEL QUESTIONS

Short Questions

1. Define the term 'market'.
2. What is price Leadership?
3. What is Product Differentiation?
4. Define the term Oligopoly.
5. Differentiate between collusive oligopoly and non-collusive oligopoly.
6. Differentiate between monopoly and monopolistic competition.
7. Give the meaning of perfect competition.
8. What is monopolistic competition?

Essay Questions

1. How is price determined under a monopoly situation?
2. Selling cost and product differentiation play an important role in monopolistic competition. Explain.
3. Explain the features of perfect competition.
4. What is the role of time element in price determination in a perfect market?
5. Write a short note on: (a) dumping, (b) price discrimination.
6. Differenciate between collusive and non-collusive oligopoly and how it is related to the hotel industry?

10

Pricing Policy

10.1. MEANING

Pricing of a product plays a very important role for the entrepreneur as it helps him to obtain a certain percentage of profit as a reward for his risk bearing and accurate decision making. Pricing is an important device for the firm to expand its market.

Pricing policy refers to the policy followed by a firm when it is fixing a price for its commodity. Also referred to as a 'set of rules' adopted by a firm or public enterprise which determine price. The main aim of an enterprise or firm is to maximize its profits and also maximize its sales. But if the firm wants to maximize its sales, it cannot increase the price of its product. This is because if the price is increased the demand for the commodity falls. On the other hand when price is decreased the demand for that particular product goes down, the sales might increase, but after some time it might gradually fall if the competitors follow suit. Therefore a suitable pricing policy should be fixed so that the sales are also maintained and also by, which profits are obtained.

10.2. GENERAL CONSIDERATIONS INVOLVED IN PRICING

Prevailing market price: Price policy should be set according to competitive situation prevailing in the market. If the firm is operating under perfect competition it acts only as a price taker, but under imperfect competition, it can set its own price policy depending upon the number, size of the product and the products of different competitors in the market. It also depends on the possibility of new firms entering the market and the stage of the consumer accepting the product.

Goal of profit and sales: Pricing policy should be able to stimulate both profit and sales. when the firms seek to maximize profits as well as sales. Sales should be more profit oriented than loss, as it initiates the producer to stay in the business.

Conflicting interests of people involved in business: The interest of the manufacturer and middlemen differ when fixing the price. The manufacturer offers a lower margin to his commodities than that of the middlemen. But the middlemen would inturn sell at a larger margin. The manufacturer also wants to curtail the middlemen's commission and reduce the retail price of the product. these conflicting motive of individuals who are involved at different chains affect the pricing of a product.

Product and promotional policies: Pricing is considered to be the only one aspect of market strategies and a firm must consider it together with its product and promotional policies. Thus before making a price change, the firm must be sure that its price fetches a good demand with its customers.

10.3. OBJECTIVES OF PRICING

The firms overall objectives serve as guiding principles to pricing. Thus the firm's business objectives are normally the objectives of a firm's price policy.

1. ***Maximization of profits:*** Maximization of profits is considered to be the main objective of a firm's price policy. The prices determined by the entrepreneurs are such that the firms obtain maximum revenue.
2. ***Survival:*** Basically in a monopolistic market situation the firm is always interested in the continued survival. For the sake of surviving in a competitive situation, a firm is ready to tolerate upheavals in the production line, organizational and in various areas of production.
3. ***Price stability:*** The firms may be willing to keep the prices of a commodity stable for a long period of time. To fulfill this objective the prices of commodities has to remain constant over a period of time. They should not fluctuate within a very short period. A stable price policy brings in sufficient profits also.

4. ***Preventing competition:*** In pricing a particular commodity, the firm may check a rival's entry through lowering its price, so as to prevent competition from the new firms.
5. ***Capturing the market:*** Another very important objective of pricing policy of a firm in business is to capture the market. The seller time and again tries to change his price for the product depending upon the consumer's demand for the product and the main motive of a seller may not be profit maximization and sales optimization, but also to capture the market through his sales and also to widen his area of selling, which inturn would obtain for him a better name and also a bright prospect for his commodities.
6. ***Achieving the target:*** The firms determine a price with a view to achieve the sales target. The producers fix a price, which could bring suitable returns for their investment. Therefore if the producers want to reach the target they have to fix a reasonable price.

10.4. FACTORS INVOLVED IN PRICING POLICY

Pricing is a complex phenomenon and depends on both the internal and external factors. Normally pricing depends on the objectives of the business, competitions in the market. Price sensitivity, quality of the customers, government interference.

The broad factors involving pricing decisions are:

1. ***Costs:*** costs plays an important role in pricing decisions. Price has to be along cost. Cost may be affected due to increase in the price of raw materials, taxes, promotional expenditure, wages, packaging, establishment charges etc. Costs are also affected due to increase in the volume of business and this is affected by price in the market. To take business decisions in the short run, variable cost have greater relevance. Economy in cost of production is important for setting a lower price and a higher cost of production leads to a higher price for the product.
2. ***Demand:*** Demand for a commodity depends on the consumer' s preference. The consumers psychology helps in changing prices in different markets and thereby earning profits. If the demand for the product is inelastic, the policy

of increasing the price would prove profitable. On the other hand, if the demand is elastic, a policy of reducing price would prove profitable. Thus pricing depends on the demand for the product and also elasticity of the demand.

3. ***Competition:*** The nature of pricing largely depends on the competitive situation prevailing in the market. Under perfect competition, there is uniform price, and the firm is in no position to fix its own price policy. On the other hand, in imperfect competition, depending on the competitive situation in the market, the firms can determine their own price policy.
4. ***Profits:*** Profit acts as seed money for future investments. Thus in determining the price of a commodity profit plays a major role. Since the goal of business is mainly to make profits, it plays an important role for the survival in business. Most of the time, producers like to stick to their price, this may be to avoid competition, or as an act of sales promotion.
5. ***Government policy:*** The fiscal policy, taxation policy of the government also play a predominant role in price fixation. For instance in case of harmful commodities, like tobacco, drugs the government levies a high percentage of tax, to prevent the production of these commodities or prevent the use of the same.

10.5. DIFFERENT METHODS OF PRICING

The traditional method of determining the price depending on the supply and the demand of the commodity is of little use to modern business men. Since they do not intend to close business within a very short period of time, they would take various factors into account before deciding on fixing the price for the commodity. Since the non economic factors like competitors, market situation, government policy play a vital role in pricing, it is seen that the economic formula of MR = MC in fixing the output and price does not work always.

The various pricing methods employed by businessmen are:

- Cost plus pricing or full cost pricing
- Pricing for a rate of return
- Marginal cost pricing

- Going rate policy
- Administered prices.

*1. **Cost Plus Pricing or full cost pricing:*** This method is also called the margin pricing or the mark up pricing. Under this method cost is estimated and a percentage of profit is added to it. Here price is set to cover all costs (all inputs involved in production process) and a predetermined percentage of profit is added to it. The percentages added to the cost are called margins or mark-ups. This percentage can differ from one firm to another firm depending on the product produced. For example the accommodation fare may differ from one five star hotel to another, though they belong to the star same category.

Cost plus pricing = cost + fair profit.

The advantages include:

- It helps in setting a fair price for the product.
- It is easy for application to all types of firms.
- All businessmen within the industry adopt it.
- Helps against price wars and severe competition.
- It is best while dealing with uncertainty and ignorance.

The drawbacks of this method are:

- It ignores consumer's preference and demand.
- It takes one sided approach.
- It fails to reflect the forces of competition adequately.
- Cost of producing the product plays a vital role in fixing the price, than the other factors.
- It only uses the average cost.
- It over stresses the precision of allocated costs.

*2. **Rate of return pricing:*** This method is also called **target pricing**. Under this method, the manufacturer considers a pre-determined target rate of return on capital invested. The pricing policy is determined along a rate of planned return. The rate of return is then translated in to percent of mark-up. Determined on the normal rate of production, the total cost of year's normal production is estimated and regarded as standard cost. Then the capital turnover is computed by taking the ratio on invested capital to the annual standard cost. The mark-up percentage of profit is obtained by multiplying capital turnover by the goal rate of return.

The percentage of the mark-up cost can be calculated as:

$$\textbf{Percentage markup on cost} = \frac{\textbf{Capital employed}}{\textbf{Total annual cost}} \times \textbf{planned rate of return}$$

3. Marginal cost pricing: In this method, the price is fixed on the basis of the marginal costs or the variable cost. The fixed cost is completely ignored in the short run, as it is fixed and their importance becomes very limited, hence the variable cost is taken into account. The firm uses marginal cost, which is directly attributable to the output of the product during a specific period. Price based on the marginal cost is more aggressive.

Advantages

- Marginal cost pricing is useful for public utility undertakings. It helps them to use maximum capacity and also to increase production. This can be adopted when a lower price is charged for the product, which in turn maximizes social welfare.
- Marginal cost pricing is ideal over the life cycle of a product.
- This method also helps in utilizing the resources to the optimum level possible.
- It also helps the firms to face the competitive situation, for instance the export markets fix their prices based on this method, since the international market is more competitive in nature.

Limitations

- During times cyclical business depressions, the firms find it difficult to employ this method of pricing. This is because of a fall in demand for commodities, which leads to an inevitable decrease in price.
- It is also said pricing under marginal costs would lead to deficits. This is because under decreasing costs, marginal cost pricing, is unsuitable.
- The management personnel should be fully aware of the techniques of the marginal cost pricing before they employ it. Hence the marginal cost requires a better understanding of it application.

4. Going rate policy: It is a policy of the firm wherein the firm adjusts its own price policy to the general price structure in the industry. Though the firm has complete freedom to fix its own price, it will not do so, instead it tries to adjust its own price policy with the price prevailing in the market. Under this method the firms fix the price for their product depending on the current price prevailing in the market. This method is also called the acceptance pricing. The firms tries to determine the lowest price that the seller can afford to accept considering various alternatives.

The going rate policy is adopted when costs are difficult to measure and the firms want to avoid tension of price rivalry in the market. This phenomenon is operated under oligopoly and duopoly situation.

Advantages

- It helps in preventing the severe competition between firms.
- It is a rational pricing method when costs are difficult to measure.
- It is suitable to avoid price hazards in oligopoly market.

It is also noted that going rate pricing is not the same as accepting the market price as in a perfect market. In the perfect market the firms are only price takers, where as in this case the firm haa some power to set it its own price, if it is willing to face adverse consequences of its decision. However it plays a safe role in following others. Hence it is also called **imitative pricing**.

5. Administered Pricing Administered prices are the prices of commodities fixed by the government to prevent unnecessary price escalations, black marketing and shortages in supply. The government resort to administered prices for essential raw materials like steel, cement, fertilizers. Indian economists have defined administered prices as 'price for a commodity which is decided arbitrarily by the government rather than determined by the market mechanism'. Administered prices are the results of the government intervention, they are prescribed by the government rather than by the market mechanism. They are normally set by on the basis of cost plus a stipulated margin of profit. Where there is a change in the costs of production, the administered price will also be changed. But this change in administered price will not be proportional to the costs incurred and these changes in prices will be delayed.

The main characteristics are:

- They are fixed by the government.
- They are fixed on certain essential commodities.
- They are statutory in nature and legally enforced by the government.
- They are also regulatory in nature.
- They are said to be outcome of the price policy of the government.

Need for administered prices:

- To check undesirable price rise, of essential commodities and raw materials especially when their demand outstrips their supply.
- To correct the imperfections of the market mechanism and lopsidedness in price structure of the free enterprise. It is seen that most of the time assumptions of perfect competition do not hold good. Thus to ensure full employment of resources or on equitable distribution of income. Administered prices is needed.
- To check undue increase of prices of certain goods when their demand outstrips their supply.
- To provide essential commodities of mass consumption at low subsided prices to the poorer sections.
- The check the monopolists from charging very high prices on their commodities.
- It also checks increasing growth of the market demand against the slow pace of the growth of market supply.

The pricing policy plays an important role for the firm. Since price fixation also affects the profit making of the firm, prices should be so fixed that it suits the consumer interests. It is thus seen that any kind of business whether it is producing agrabathis to the complicated electronic goods to the production of food items in a restaurant or a hotel, pricing the commodity plays a very important role. Accurate pricing not only brings in more profits, it helps the entrepreneur to expand or even diversify his business and it also acts as a seed money for further reinvestment in his business.

MODEL QUESTIONS

Short Questions

1. What are administered prices?
2. Explain the term marginal cost pricing.
3. What is meant by pricing policy?
4. State in brief the objectives of a firm.

Essay Questions

1. Explain the various factors, which influence the pricing of a commodity.
2. What are the various methods of pricing?

APPENDIX I

Tourism has several dimensions other than economic among them the complex of interactions and their consequences that occur before curing and after a tourist trip. There are also psychological, sociological, ecological and political travel impacts.

Job descriptions are available for many of the businesses. In 1994 the couscil on Hotel, restaurant and institutional education (CHRIE) along with the convocation of National hospitality and tourism association published 117 model position descriptions that include hotel and restaurant jobs plus few other from the field of tourism.

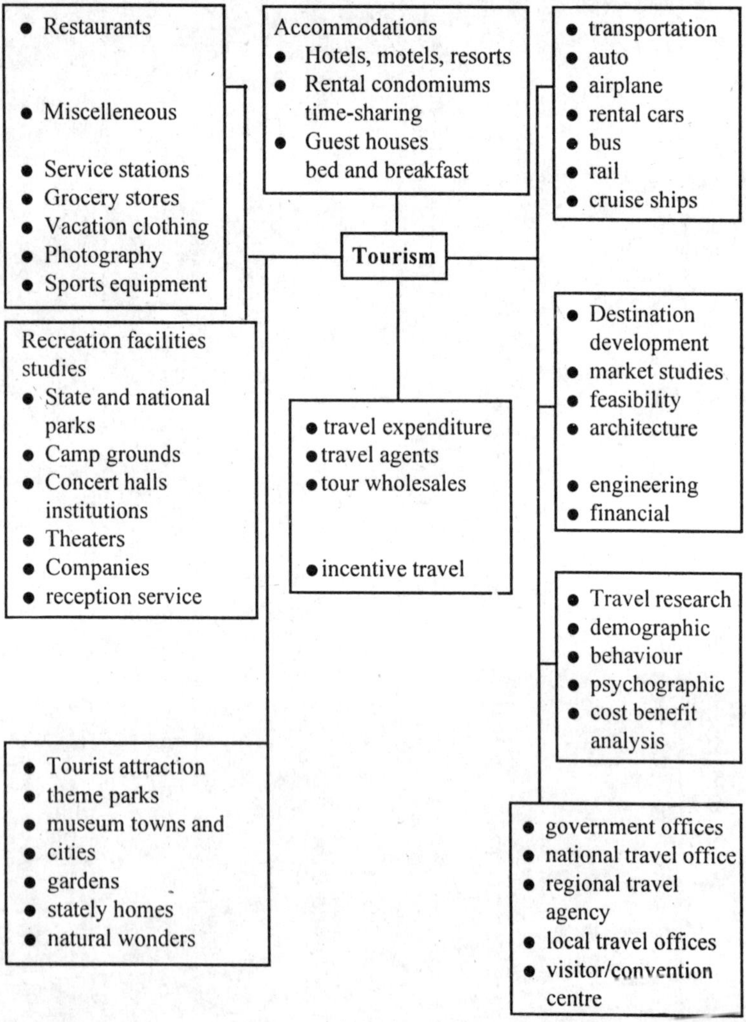

APPENDIX II

The tourism industry consists of several interconnected businesses. The below show an example of the Canadian tourism industry which comprises of around 6000 business.

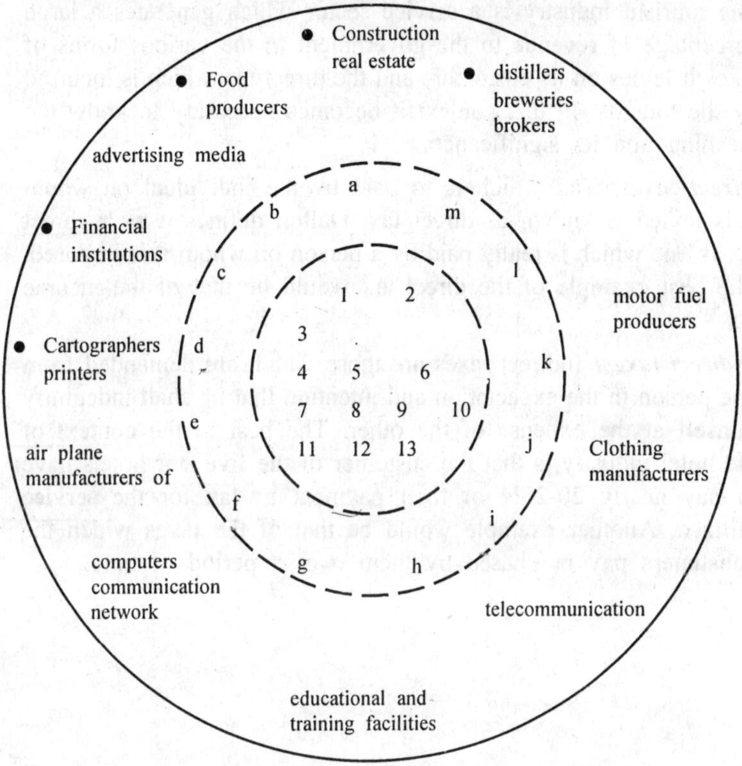

Tourism in Canada

1. transportation	a. hotel and restaurant supplies
2. accomodation	b. telecommunication
3. food and beverage	c. serivce stations
4. attraction	d. credit cards banking service
5. camping	e. retailers shopping works
6. fising	f. reservation system
7. travel agencies	g. museums, theatres
8. tours companies	h. auto clubs
9. souvenirs	i. Parks recreational centres
10. travellers cheques	j. sporting events

11.	hunting equipment	k.	camera film
12.	luggage	l.	maps, travel books
13.	car rentals	m.	museum cultural activities, theatres.

The tourism industry is a service sector which generates a large percentage of revenue to the government in the various forms of taxes it levies on its customers and the direct tax which is incurred by the tourists. In this context it becomes necessary to know the meaning and its significance.

Direct taxes: Tax which is to paid by the individual on whom it is levied is known as direct tax. Dalton defines it as 'a direct tax is one which is really paid by a person on whom it is imposed. The best example of the direct tax would be that of the income tax.

Indirect taxes: Indirect taxes are those which are demanded from one person in the expectation and intention that he shall indemnify himself at the expense of the other. The best in the context of the hotel industry is that the customer of the five star hotels have to pay nearly 20-25% of their payment as tax for the service utilized. Another example would be that of the taxes which the consumers pay purchased by them over a period of time.

APPENDIX III

National Income Concepts

The national income does not speak of the income of a particular country during a period of time. It speaks of the contribution of the various sectors to the economy during a specific period of time which is usually a year. The tourism industry and its subsidiary industry which is the hotel industry obtains for the government for a government a sizeable percentage of the GDP and Personal income. Here it becomes essential, to understand the basic concepts of national income.

Gross National Product: The basic social accounting measure, it is the nation's total production of goods and services, usually for one year, evaluated in terms of the market price. In calculating the GNP the final value of goods and services produced in the country is taken into account. Intermediate goods are excluded from accounting in order to avoid double counting. In calculating the gross national product the depreciation or the replacement of fixed asset is not taken into account.

Net National Product (NNP): It refers to the net production of goods and services in a country in a year. It is the GNP minus the depreciation. It is also called the national income at market price. It is highly useful concept in the study of growth economics as it takes into consideration the net increase in the total production of the country.

National income at factor cost: the total income of all payments received by the factors of production land, labour, capital and organization. It can be summarized as follows:

National income at factor cost = NNP – indirect taxes = subsidies.

Personal income: the actual income received by the individuals or households in the country during a year.

Personal income = national income – corporate income taxes – undistributed corporate profits – social contributions + transfer payments.

Gross domestic product: the sum of goods and services produced in a year with in the country is known as gross domestic product. The international transactions which are carried out in the form of export and imports and payments made or received are not calculated in the gross domestic product.

Disposable personal income: the entire personal income is not available to individuals for consumption as they have to pay personal direct taxes. That part of personal income, which is left behind after payment of personal direct taxes, is called disposable personal income. DPI = PI — personal direct taxes.
It can also be written as Disposal personal income = consumption + savings.

Per capita income: the per capital income is the income per head or it can stated as the average income of the individuals in the country. It indicates the standard of living of people of a country during a period of time.

It can be calculated as national income divided by the no of population.

I BHM Examination, October/November 2001
(New Scheme)
ECONOMICS
Hotel Economics and Statistics – I (Paper – I)

Time : 3 Hours Max. Marks : 90

SECTION – A

I. Answer any ten sub-questions in not exceeding three sentences each. Each sub-question carries 2 marks. (10 × 2 = 20)

a) What are the different kinds of Hotels ?
b) Explain the term 'Balance of Payments'.
c) Distinguish between total utility and marginal utility.
d) What is meant by consumer's sovereignty ?
e) Define demand.
f) What is duopoly ?
g) Define cross elasticity of demand.
h) Distinguish between supply and production.
i) What is opportunity cost ?
j) State the law of variable proportions.
k) What are selling costs ?
l) What is an envelop curve ?
m) What do you mean by equilibrium of industry ?
n) What is price leadership ?
o) What is monopolistic competition ?

SECTION – B

II. Answer any six questions in not exceeding one page each. Each question carries five marks. (6 × 5 = 30)

2. Explain the concept of consumer's surplus.
3. What is short-term demand forecasting ? State its objectives.

4. State briefly the importance of price elasticity of den and in hotel industry.
5. Describe the features of Iso-quants.
6. What are the determinants of supply in Hotel Industry ?
7. What are the features of perfect competition ?
8. What are the features of tourism ?
9. What is pricing policy ? Explain various considerations involved in pricing policy.

SECTION – C

III. Answer any four of the following questions in not exceeding two pages each. Each question carries ten marks.

(4 × 10 = 40)

10. Discuss the importance of Hotel Industry in Indian Economy.
11. Explain consumer equilibrium with the help of indifference curve technique.
12. Explain the law of demand with necessary illustrations and a diagram.
13. Explain briefly various pricing methods.
14. Discuss the various types of internal economies of production.
15. Explain the influence of time element in the determination of price.

I BHM Examination, April/May 2001

(New Scheme)

ECONOMICS (Paper – I)

(Hotel Economics and Statistics – I)

Time : 3 Hours Max. Marks : 90

SECTION – A

I. Answer any ten sub-questions in not exceeding three sentences each. Each sub-question carries 2 marks. (10 × 2 = 20)

a) What is a trend line ?
b) What is meant by domestic tourism ?
c) Define cross elasticity of demand.
d) What do you understand by demand forecasting ?
e) What are selling costs ?
f) Define 'indifference map'.
g) Distinguish between 'total utility' and 'marginal utility'
h) What do you mean by 'Palace on Wheels'?
i) Why short-run cost curves are U-shaped ?
j) What is duopoly ?
k) State the law of variable proportions.
l) What is elasticity of supply ?
m) Define product differentiation.
n) What is price leadership ?
o) Distinguish between 'extension of demand' and 'increase in demand'.

SECTION – B

II. Answer any six questions in not exceeding one page each. Each question carries five marks. (6 × 5 = 30)

2. What are the limitations to consumer's sovereignty ?

3. Explain the law of equi-marginal utility.
4. What are the exceptions to the law of demand ?
5. What are the features of a good demand forecasting method?
6. What are the features of monopoly market ?
7. Briefly state the factors which determine elasticity of demand in hotel industry.
8. Distinguish between cost plus method of pricing and pricing for a rate of return.
9. What are the properties of indifference curves ?

SECTION – C

III. Answer any four of the following questions in not exceeding two pages each. Each question carries ten marks.

(4 × 10 = 40)

10. Discuss the contribution of Hotel Industry to the rest of the Economy.
11. Analyse the concept of consumers surplus with the help of suitable examples and a diagram.
12. Explain the influence of time element in the determination of price.
13. What are Iso-quant and Iso-cost curves ? Show how a producer reaches the position of equilibrium with the help of Iso-quant and Iso-cost curves.
14. Analyse the cost concepts relevant to hotel industry.
15. What is pricing policy ? Explain the different factors involved in the pricing policy of a firm.

I BHM Examination, April/May 2001
(Old Scheme)
HOTEL ECONOMICS AND STATISTICS – I (Paper – I)

Time : 3 Hours Max. Marks : 90

SECTION – A

I. Answer any six sub-questions in not more than 6 lines each. Each sub-question carries 3 marks. (6 × 3 = 18)

a) Define tourism.

b) What are the kinds of hotels ?

c) What do you mean by 'Palace on Wheels' ?

d) What is demand projection ?

e) Define selling costs.

f) Distringuish between 'Balance of Trade' and 'Balance of Payments'.

g) What is kinked demand curve ?

h) What is monopolistic competition ?

i) What are 'Giffen goods' ?

j) Differentiate /between firm and industry.

SECTION – B

II. Answer any three questions. Each question carries 6 marks. (3 × 6 = 18 marks)

2. Analyse the role of government in Hotel Industry in India.
3. Differentiate between 'extension and contraction' of demand and 'increase and decrease' in demand.
4. Analyse the cost concepts relevant to Hotel Industry.
5. What are the determinants of demand ?
6. Explain the growth of tourism in India.

SECTION – C

III. Answer any three questions. Each question carries 18 marks. (3 × 18 = 54 marks)

7. Analyse the importance of Hotel Industry.
8. What are the features of perfect competition ? Explain how price is determined under perfect competition.
9. Define 'elasticity of demand'. Explain the different types of elasticity of demand.
10. What is simple monopoly ? How would you determine price and output in such a situation in hotel industry ?
11. What is demand forecasting ? Mention various methods of demand forecasting.

I BHM Degree Examination, Oct./Nov. 2000
(New Scheme)
HOTEL ECONOMICS AND STATISTICS – I (Paper – I)

Time : 3 Hours Max. Marks : 90

***Instruction** : Answer to all questions should be written in English only.*

SECTION – A

I. Answer any six sub-questions from this section in not more than 6 lines each. Each sub-question carries 3 marks. (6 × 3 = 18)

a) What are 'selling costs' ?
b) What do you mean by 'Giffin's Paradox' ?
c) What is 'Price Leadership' ?
d) What do you mean by 'Palace on Wheels' ?
e) Explain the term 'Balance of Payments'.
f) What is 'Price discrimination' ?
g) What is 'Duopoly' ?
h) What is 'Income Elasticity of Demand' ?
i) Distinguish between 'Fixed Cost' and 'Variable Cost'.
j) What is 'Foreign Tourism' ?

SECTION – B

II. Answer any three questions from this Section. Each question carries 6 marks. (3 × 6 = 18)

2. What is 'Oligopoly' ? Explain its features.
3. What are the general features of perfect competition ?
4. What are the factors that determine the demand for hotel industry ?
5. Explain the shape of long-run average cost curve. How is it derived ?

6. Briefly explain the various degrees of price elasticity of demand.

SECTION – C

III. Answer any three questions from this Section. Each question carries 18 marks. (3 × 18 = 54 marks)

7. What is monopolistic competition ? How would you determine price and output in such a situation in hotel industry ? Explain with the help of diagrams.
8. Explain the role of Government in hotel industry in India.
9. What is simple 'Monopoly' ? How would you determine price and output in such a situation ? Explain with the help of diagrams.
10. Discuss the contribution of the hotel industry to the rest of the economy.
11. Briefly explain various methods of demand projection with reference to hotel industry.

I BHM Degree Examination, April/May 2000
(New Scheme)
HOTEL ECONOMICS AND STATISTICS (Paper – I)

Time : 3 Hours   Max. Marks : 90

Instruction : *Answer to all questions should be written in English only.*

SECTION – A

I. Answer any six sub-questions from this section in not more than 6 lines each. Each question carries 3 marks. (6 × 3 = 18)

a) What is demand ?
b) What is 'Motel' ?
c) What is meant by 'extension' and 'contraction' of demand ?
d) What is 'Opportunity cost' ?
e) What is 'product differentiation' ?
f) What is 'Griffen's Paradox ?
g) What is 'Oligopoly' ?
h) What is 'Discriminating Monopoly' ?
i) What is 'Price elasticity of demand'?
j) What is 'Price elasticity of demand' ?

SECTION – B

II. Answer any three questions from this Section. Each question carries 6 marks. (3 × 6 = 18)

2. What do you mean by "home on wheels"? Explain its importance in "Indian Tourism".
3. Expansion of Hotel Industry can significantly solve "India's Balance of Payments" difficulties. Explain.

4. What are the various determinants of demand for hotel industry in India ?
5. What is Cross Price Elasticity of Demand ? Explain the cross Elasticity for various goods which are related to each other.
6. What is Monopoly ? Explain the different types of monopoly conditions in Indian Industries.

SECTION – C

III. Answer any three questions from this Section. Each question carries 18 marks. (3 × 18 = 54)

7. What is "Cost-Volume-Output" analysis ? Explain the relationship among cost volume and output in hotel industry.
8. What is "Perfect Competition"? Explain its features. Explain the short-run and long-run conditions of equilibrium under perfectly competitive market situations.
9. Give a brief account of various facilities provided by the hotels to the public.
10. Give an account of the growth and development of Hotel Industry in India.
11. What are the various methods of "Demand Forecasting"? Explain.

Ist Year B.H.M. Examination, Nov./Dec. 1999
(New Scheme)
HOTEL MANAGEMENT
Hotel Economics and Statistics – I

Time : 3 Hours   Max. Marks : 90

SECTION – A

I. Answer any six sub-questions from this section in not more than 6 lines each. Each sub-question carries 3 marks. (6 × 3 = 18)

a) Define the term "Demand".
b) What is Foreign Tourism ?
c) What is oligopoly ?
d) What is opportunity cost ?
e) What do you mean by 'Home on wheels'?
f) Who is 'Fit-Free-Independent Traveller' ?
g) What is 'Balance of payments' ?
h) What is 'product defferentiation' ?
i) What is 'unitary elastic demand' ?
j) What is 'price leadership' ?

SECTION – B

II. Answer any 3 questions. Each question carries 6 marks. (3 × 6 = 18 marks)

2. Discuss the importance of Hotel Industry in Indian Economy.
3. Explain the features of perfect competition.
4. Briefly explain any two methods of Demand projection with reference to Hotel Industry.
5. Explain the methods of determining price and output in Hotel Industry.
6. What do you mean by opportunity cost ? Show its relevance in Managerial decision making.

SECTION – C

III. Answer any 3 questions. Each question carries 18 marks. (3 × 18 = 54)

7. Define 'Monopoly'. Explain how price and output are determined under Monopoly situation.
8. What is 'elasticity of Demand' ? Explain the various types of Elasticity of Demand.
9. Give an account of the growth and development of Hotel Industry in India.
10. Discuss and evaluate the mechanism of price determination under conditions of 'perfect competition'.
11. Give a brief account of the various facilities provided by the hotels to the public.

1st Year B.H.M. Examination, April/May 1999
(New Scheme)
HOTEL ECONOMICS AND STATISTICS (Paper – I)

Time : 3 Hours Max. Marks : 90

Instruction : *Answer to all questions should be written in English only.*

SECTION – A

I. Answer any six sub-questions from this section in not more than 6 lines each. Each sub-question carries 3 marks. (6 × 3 = 18)

a) What is "Market Experimentation"?
b) What are the different kinds of hotels ?
c) What are selling costs ?
d) What is Demand projection ?
e) What is 'Giffens paradox' ?
f) What is 'price leadership' ?
g) What is real cost ?
h) What do you mean by "palace on wheels" ?
i) Define Tourism.
j) What is a 'trend line' ?

SECTION – B

II. Answer any three questions. Each question carries 6 marks. (3 × 6 = 18 marks)

2. Explain the various exceptions to the Law of Demand.
3. "Expansion of Hotel Industry can significantly solve India's Balance of payments difficulties". Explain.
4. Explain different concepts of cost in Hotel Industry.
5. Write a note on the various determinants of demand for hotel and catering services.

6. Explain the relationship between cost, volume and output in hotel industry.

SECTION – C

III. Answer any three questions. Each question carries 18 marks. $(3 \times 18 = 54)$

7. Define Elasticity of Demand. Explain the different types of elasticity of Demand.
8. What is Monopolistic competition ? How would you determine price and output in Hotel Industry in a Monopolistic competitive situation ?
9. Discuss the contribution of Hotel Industry to the rest of the Economy.
10. What is Oligopoly ? What are the different kinds of Oligopoly ?
11. Evaluate the fiscal and monetary policies of the Government of India towards Hotel Industry in India.

I B.H.M. Degree Examination, Oct./Nov. 1998
(New Scheme)
ECONOMICS
Hotel Economics and Statistics – I

Time : 3 Hours Max. Marks : 90

SECTION – A

I. Answer any six sub-questions from this section in not more than 6 lines each. Each question carries 3 marks. (6 × 3 = 18)

a) What is Domestic Tourism ?
b) What is Law of Demand ?
c) Differentiate 'Firm' and 'Industry'.
d) What are the different kinds of Hotels ?
e) What is 'Oligopoly' ?
f) What are 'Selling Costs' ?
g) What is 'Balance of Payments' ?
h) What is 'Opportunity Costs' ?
i) Who is 'Fit-Free-Independent Traveller' ?
j) What is 'Price-leadership' ?

SECTION – B

II. Answer any three questions. Each question carries 6 marks. (3 × 6 = 18 marks)

2. Explain different concepts of costs in Hotel Industry.
3. Explain the features of perfect competition.
4. Explain the importance of Hotel Industry in Indian Economy.
5. What are the factors that determine Elasticity of demand in Hotel Industry ?
6. What are the exceptions to the Law of Demand ?

SECTION – C

III. Answer any three questions. Each question carries 18 marks. (3 × 18 = 54)

7. Explain the growth of the Hotel Industry in India in comparison with the Indian Economy.
8. What is Demand analysis ? Explain the different Demand projection methods for the products of Hotel Industry.
9. What is Monopolistic competition ? How would you determine price and output in hotel industry in a monopolistic competitive situation ?
10. What is Elasticity of demand ? Explain the Price, Income and Cross Elasticity of Demand.
11. "Selling Costs and product differentiation are the hall-marks in Monopolistic market" – Explain.

I B.H.M. Degree Examination, April 1998
(New Scheme)
HOTEL ECONOMICS
Hotel Economics and Statistics – I

Time : 3 Hours Max. Marks : 90

SECTION – A

I. Answer any 6 sub-questions from this section in not more than 6 lines each. Each question carries 3 marks.

(6 × 3 = 18)

a) What is Domestic Tourism ?
b) What is Demand ?
c) What is a 'Motel' ?
d) What is 'Sample Survey' ?
e) Explain the term 'Balance of Payments'.
f) What is 'Price-leadership' ?
g) What do you mean by 'Palace on Wheels' ?
h) What are 'Selling costs' ?
i) Differentiate 'Fixed costs' & 'Variable Costs'.
j) What is meant by 'extension' and 'contraction' of demand ?

SECTION – B

II. Answer any 3 questions. Each question carries 6 marks.

(3 × 6 = 18 marks)

2. Discuss the importance of Hotel Industry in Indian Economy.
3. What are the different methods of demand projection in hotel industry ?
4. Explain the general features of perfect competition.
5. Explain the role of Government in Hotel industry in India.
6. What is cross Elasticity of demand ? Explain with reference to substitutes and complementaries.

SECTION – C

III. Answer any three questions. Each question carries 18 marks. (3 × 18 = 54)

7. "The success of Tourism largely depends upon political peace, political harmony, civil order and efficient police" — explain.
8. What is simple monopoly ? How would you determine price and output in such a situation in hotel industry ?
9. What is Elasticity of demand ? Explain how the knowledge of elasticity of demand for hotel and catering services might be of use to hoteliers and caterers/
10. "Selling costs and product differentiation are the hall-marks in monopolistic market". Explain.
11. Give an account of the growth and development of hotel industry in India.